Coping with America

Drawing by Sempé © C. Charillon, Paris

Coping with America

Peter Trudgill

Basil Blackwell

© Peter Trudgill 1982; 1985

First published 1982
Reprinted 1982
Second edition 1985
Second edition reprinted and first published in paperback 1987

Basil Blackwell Ltd
108 Cowley Road, Oxford OX4 1JF, UK

Basil Blackwell Inc.
432 Park Avenue South, Suite 1503, New York, NY 10016, USA

British Library Cataloguing in Publication Data
Trudgill, Peter
    Coping with America: a beginner's guide to the U.S.A. —
    2nd ed.
    1. United States — Handbooks, manuals, etc.
    I. Title.
    917.3'04927   E158

    ISBN 0−631−14324−6
    ISBN 0−631−15442−6

Library of Congress Cataloging in Publication Data
Trudgill, Peter.
    Coping with America.
    Includes index.
    1. United States — Handbooks, manuals, etc.
    I. Title.
    E158.T78   1985   917.3'04927   85−3981

    ISBN 0−631−14324−6
    ISBN 0−631−15442−6

Typeset by Cambrian Typesetters, Frimley
Printed in Great Britain by Billing and Sons Ltd, Worcester

For Jean, my favourite American

Contents

Preface to the Second Edition — viii

Introduction — ix

Acknowledgements — xii

Getting There and Getting Back — 1

Money — 5

Geography, Climate and other Natural Hazards — 12

Making Telephone Calls — 20

Hiring and Driving a Car — 26

Transport and Travel — 42

Hotels and Motels — 52

Eating . . . — 56

. . . and Drinking — 73

In the City — 79

Mail — 84

Shopping — 87

At Home with Americans — 92

TV and Radio — 100

Quaint Institutions and Customs — 105

Watching and Understanding Sport — 113

Being Ill and Keeping Healthy — 128

Language: Understanding and Being Understood — 132

Units of Measurement and Sizes — 136

Meeting American People — 139

Index — 141

Suggestions — 145

Preface to the Second Edition

This second edition of *Coping with America* represents an attempt to bring the book up to date by incorporating information on those aspects of fast-moving American society that have changed since the publication of the first edition. Interestingly, I have also had to take note of changes in European society, where the Americanization of certain aspects of our lives has made one or two pieces of advice contained in the first edition unnecessary. The text of this edition has benefited, I hope, from the suggestions, observations, corrections, insights and information provided by the many, many people who have written to the publishers to share with me their experiences of coping with America. If the second edition is not an improvement on the first, it is not their fault. I am very grateful to all of them, but especially to those correspondents who wrote extended commentaries on the book. Of those who clearly devoted hours of their lives to help me, and everybody else, cope better next time, I would particularly like to thank James R. Solomon and Christopher Derrick. I would also like to acknowledge the assistance of the many magnanimous Americans who wrote with updates, anecdotes and just plain facts. Not one of these kind people had a cross word to say about ignorant foreigners. I am very grateful for their forbearance, and for their help.

P.T.
January 1985

Introduction

This is not a guidebook in the normal sense of the word. It does not tell you what to see, which places to visit, where to stay or how much anything costs. For information of that sort other guidebooks can be consulted. What this book tries to do is to provide you with the sort of information that cannot be found in traditional guidebooks to the USA, which are mostly written by (and for) Americans, who have no way of knowing what aspects of life in their country can come as problems or surprises to the foreign visitor. I have tried to give the first-time foreign, and particularly European, visitor to the USA information on how to do things, what to say and what to expect in different situations. The USA is not a difficult country to get along in, but in many ways it is not, as yet, geared to catering for foreign visitors, though individual Americans are enormously helpful to people they recognize as foreign — so do ask for help if you need it. The USA is also a surprisingly foreign country even to, say, Britons and Australians, who speak the same language.

I am not a professional expert on the United States. A full-time expert would probably not have been able to write a book of this sort. I wrote this book after having spent a year in America. This is long enough to have come to an appreciation of how things are done in the USA — although I would never have dared to write it without the help and collaboration of many American friends — but not long enough to have forgotten how difficult things can be at first when one is newly arrived in a foreign land. The book contains the sort of advice and information I found myself giving to recently arrived compatriots and other foreign friends who came to visit me during that year, so that they would be able to cope with America on their own. But there are bound to be subjects I have neglected or overlooked, and I would be glad to hear from anyone who has ideas for improving the book. There is a form for this purpose on page 145.

Readers whose suggestions I adopt will receive a free copy of any future edition.

A danger with a book like this, which sets out to describe the characteristics and customs of an enormous and diverse land, is that generalizations are likely to be less than totally accurate. What is true of some parts of the country, or of some social or ethnic groups, may not be true of others. I have tried to take this into account in the text, but although I have visited forty-one of the forty-eight mainland states, I am naturally better acquainted with some areas than others. Any Americans reading this book are therefore asked to be charitable about what may seem to them like misrepresentations.

They are also asked to forgive what will probably appear to them to be exaggerations: if this book is full of tornadoes, cockroaches, guns and hamburgers, it is because it is things like these that loom large in the consciousness of the newly arrived visitor. I hope, too, that any annoyance Americans and others may feel will be tempered by the insights that this book may give them, by implication, into at least one set of British customs and prejudices.

One thing any stray American reader should be warned about is the British sense of humour. Many British people in the USA have made remarks of a teasing, ironic, tongue-in-cheek sort — only to find that Americans have taken them seriously and have even, therefore, taken offence. British visitors to America are warned to be careful about this, while American, Japanese and other non-British readers of this book are warned that there are a number of remarks of this sort in the following pages. Please believe that if I write that the USA is unfit for human habitation, this is not because I actually think that the USA is unfit for human habitation.

I have not always tried to be objective in this book, and my personal prejudices will be quite apparent. At times, too, I have been rather critical of things American (as well as things British) — the book is, after all, about difficulties and differences. I hope I have also made it clear, however, that America, for all that it can be appalling, perplexing and frightening, can also be — and most often is — exciting, fascinating and immensely enjoyable.

Americans are some of the nicest and friendliest people on the face of the earth. If anyone doubts my sincerity in saying this, let me point out that I have an American wife and, as a consequence, an American mother-in-law and, to stretch kinship terminology somewhat, numerous American brothers-, sisters-, uncles-, aunts-, grandfathers-, and cousins-in-law. I dedicate this book to all of them, and to those Americans who, I hope, even after the publication of the book, will continue to regard themselves as my friends.

P.T.

Acknowledgements

Very many people have helped in the preparation of this book. I am particularly grateful to the following, who have read the typescript at various stages, made comments and criticisms, supplied additional information, and corrected inaccuracies: Colin Biggs, Netta Biggs, Carol Boyack, Neil Brummage, John Davey, Gae Fasold, Ralph Fasold, Georgia Green, Jean Haimson, Rosemary Hannah, David Harvey, Margaret Huxley, Peter Huxley, Chuck Kisseberth and, especially, Jean Hannah.

The menu on page 63 is from the Boar's Head Restaurant, Champaign, Illinois, and that on page 65 is from the Chutney Kitchen, Yountville, Napa Valley, California.

Getting There and Getting Back

Americans can travel to Western European countries with only a passport. This is not the case for foreign visitors to the USA. In order to travel to the USA you need an American visa. **visas**

An application form for an ordinary tourist visa can be obtained from a travel agent, at least in Britain. Instructions for filling it in are given with each form, as is the address to which the completed form should be sent. Note that you need a form for each person travelling, including children.

If you have a query about your visa application, in Britain you may dial a recorded message about visa applications, provided by the United States Embassy in London, on (01) 499-3443. If this does not answer your question, you can ring the Visa Branch itself on (01) 499-7010, but it can take a very long time to get through. They prefer you to write.

Once you have completed the form, you or your travel agent — travel agents can often do it quicker — will then have to send it to the United States Embassy, together with your passport, a passport-sized photograph, a stamped addressed envelope, and 'evidence' that you intend to return to your native land. A note explaining that you have a job/house/family/dog to come back to will usually do. You may also have to swear that your uncle is not a communist. (It doesn't matter if he is — just swear that he isn't.)

It may take up to four weeks to get the visa, though sometimes it can be much quicker or slower than that. If you are in a hurry, it is possible in Britain to go to the United States Embassy in Grosvenor Square in London — the Visa Branch is at the side of the building, in Upper Grosvenor Street — and queue up. This process is tedious and may take hours, but it *is* quicker than four weeks — but don't forget the photographs!

A tourist visa is normally valid indefinitely. This is true even after your passport has expired — you can then gain admittance to the USA by taking both your new, valid passport and the expired one containing the visa.

If you are going to the USA to work or to study, your American employer or university will normally send you the necessary forms and tell you what to do. If you are in Britain and require information about immigration, you are advised to write to the Visa Branch, United States Embassy, 5 Upper Grosvenor Street, London W1A 2JB, enclosing a stamped, addressed envelope.

health insurance

It is *essential* to take out extensive health insurance before you travel to the USA. There is no National Health Service in America, and although Americans who are taken ill in Britain and Scandinavia often receive free health care, no one in the USA has seen fit to extend reciprocal privileges to Europeans or anyone else. And medical costs in America, especially if you have to go into hospital, can be absolutely enormous. If you have a heart attack, say, you may end up owing some hospital five years' salary.

Fuller details are given in the section on health, pages 128–31.

baggage allowance

Current baggage regulations for most scheduled trans-atlantic flights are that you may take free of charge two pieces of luggage, regardless of weight, if the length + height + width of one does not exceed 65 inches (1.65 metres) and if the dimensions of the other do not exceed 55 inches (1.40 metres).

immigration

On the plane to the USA you will be given an immigration form and a customs form to fill in. (It's a good idea to have a pen and your passport handy — unless you have memorized the number, date and place of issue of your passport.)

On the immigration form there is a small space in which you are supposed to write your address in the USA, which is rather inconvenient if you are going to be travelling about the country. In that case it is best just to put down where you are staying the first night.

On arrival in the USA the immigration officer will check your visa and the immigration form. You will be given a copy of this form to keep with your passport — often they staple it in for you. You are supposed to hand this copy in when you leave the country (unless you are leaving to visit Canada or Mexico and intend to

"What the hell is 'I heart NY' supposed to mean? I see it everywhere."

Reproduced by courtesy of *Punch*

return to the USA within thirty days before going back home). This is generally done at the airline desk when you check in for your return flight, as there are usually no passport checks when you leave the USA. However, nothing terrible seems to happen if you don't hand the form in.

The immigration officer will stamp on the immigration form how long you are entitled to stay in the USA. Make sure that he or she knows how long you want to stay.

After immigration comes customs, and somewhere along the line you will be relieved of your customs form. Although there is now a red channel/green channel system as in many other countries, you still actually have to come face to face with the customs officer. You are quite likely to be asked to open your bags — perhaps American customs officers aren't as busy as those in Europe, for they certainly seem to think that they have time to do this. Keep your passport out: they

customs

give returning Americans a much harder time than visitors.

It is important to note that you are not allowed to take into the USA any fresh fruit, fresh vegetables, butter, milk, fresh meat or plants.

in transit You normally have to go through customs and immigration at your first port of entry. This means that if you are changing planes at, say, New York to go on to somewhere else, you will probably have to collect your baggage and go through the formalities there. You can then either check in your baggage again yourself or, if there is time (say, an hour) before your connecting flight, leave your bags with a 'Sky Cap' porter or at a baggage-transfer desk and they will see to it for you.

Note that in the summer it can take a long time to get through immigration and customs.

If you have to find your way from one terminal to another and it is too far to walk, there are buses — often these are free, though at New York Kennedy they are not — or you may have to take a taxi if things are too hectic (and pay through the nose). For taxis and airport buses, see page 43.

Money

The amount of money that you take with you to the USA will depend, of course, on your needs and resources, but the form in which you take it also deserves some thought.

It is a very good idea indeed to take most of your money in the form of US dollar traveller's cheques (US: 'traveler's checks'). As elsewhere in the world, in the USA traveller's cheques are much safer than cash: they are not valid without your signature, and they will be replaced if they are lost or stolen. In the USA, however, there is also the bonus that traveller's cheques can be used very much like cash. Shops, restaurants, petrol stations and hotels will accept them as if they were cash and will give you change when necessary (a very good way of topping up your supply of cash without going to a bank). You have to sign each cheque as you use it, of course, and you may also be asked to write the date and the place and name of the business on the cheque, as well as provide some identification (see pages 10, 75).

Not all businesses, though, will accept traveller's cheques. This is especially true of small, one-man establishments — and taxi drivers are usually not very keen either. An approximate rule of thumb for British travellers is that if you could possibly use an ordinary cheque in Britain, you can use a traveller's cheque in the USA. Most people, too, will be rather reluctant to take a $50 traveller's cheque for a $1 purchase. So take most of your money in the form of traveller's cheques, but include plenty of $20 or $10 cheques for use in shops, and keep some cash on you as well.

American Express and Thomas Cook traveller's cheques are among those widely used and recognized in the USA and cause no difficulties, though the latter are undoubtedly less familiar to Americans. You can get them with no problem at a bank before you leave. Remember, though, that it is only US dollar traveller's

traveller's
cheques

cheques that can be used like cash. Sterling traveller's cheques and those in other currences are equally safe, but they have to be exchanged for dollars or dollar traveller's cheques at an American bank, so for most people there is little point in getting them. Note too that changing sterling and other foreign notes or traveller's cheques for dollars is not always easy, or even possible, at smaller American banks.

credit cards If you have credit cards, take them. Credit cards are very widely used in the USA, and all the main credit cards found in Britain are also accepted in the USA.

If you use credit cards in the USA, you will normally be billed at home, in the usual way, in pounds, at something close to the current rate of exchange. Sometimes transactions can take as long as two months to reach your bill. Sometimes that is convenient.

American shop assistants and waiters are noticeably less diligent than their European equivalents at checking the signature you provide on the bill against the one on your card, and in fact it is not uncommon for people to lend their credit cards to spouses and friends, although this is officially not permitted. It is therefore particularly important to inform the credit card company *immediately* if your card is lost or stolen.

A Visa card can be used at certain banks to obtain cash. And an American Express card can be used at American Express offices in a similar way. If you are an American Express card holder, you can use a British cheque book to write a cheque in pounds, which the American Express cashier will accept and exchange for the equivalent in dollar notes and/or traveller's cheques. (Not all cashiers know that they can do this, but they can — get them to check.) American Express also has traveller's cheque dispensers (for card holders who have applied for and received a personal identification number) at some airports and other locations. You have to pay a little for these services, of course, but they can be extremely convenient. The credit card companies seem to improve their facilities of this type from time to time, so keep a look-out for further developments.

Some American petrol stations do not accept ordinary credit cards, though most do. They also accept credit cards issued by the particular oil company whose petrol they sell (for example, Philips, Amoco, Exxon, Mobil).

Many Americans carry walletfuls of these, and indeed they are said to be a good way for younger people to improve their 'credit rating'. (Oddly enough, the more things you buy on credit, the more credit-worthy you seem to become.) Most visitors will not be in the USA long enough to make it worth getting oil-company credit cards, but if you do get one, note that some oil companies specifically *permit* you to lend your card to somebody else, so be sure to watch it carefully.

cash

The dollar notes (US: bills) that you are most likely to encounter are $1, $5, $10 and $20, though there are also $2, $50 and $100 notes. Be warned that all notes, whatever their value, are *exactly the same colour and size*. It hasn't occurred to Americans that this isn't actually a very good idea, and they are not aware that there is anything unusual about this. They also seem to manage the system very well, no doubt after many years of practice. To the foreigner, however, it really is a difficulty. You have to be very careful about organizing notes in your wallet or purse and about looking at each note individually as you spend it or receive it.

There are 100 cents to the dollar. The symbol for cent is ¢. The most common coins are:

1 cent   A small copper coin. Known as a 'penny' and labelled 'one cent'.

5 cents   A silver-coloured coin, rather larger than a penny. Known as a 'nickel' and labelled 'five cents'.

10 cents   A small silver coin — smaller than a nickel, smaller even than a penny. (This is very confusing.) Known as a 'dime' and labelled 'one dime' (*not* 'ten cents').

25 cents   A silver coin not much larger than a nickel. Known as a 'quarter' and labelled 'quarter dollar'. (It is *very* easy to confuse quarters with nickels at first — and, indeed, for quite a long time after that — but note that nickels have smooth edges, while quarters have little ridges.)

The terms 'penny', 'nickel', 'dime' and 'quarter' are not slang words on a par with the British 'quid' but perfectly standard terms. This means that you have to use them and remember which is which. The hard ones to remember are *nickel* and *dime* — perhaps it's helpful to bear in mind that 'dime' and 'decimal' (each of which is related to the number 10) both start with a 'd'.

There are also half-dollar coins and two different dollar coins, which you may come across from time to time. All three are large silver coins. Dollar coins are particularly common in Las Vegas, where they are frequently used in gambling (see page 108).

If you want to sound like a proper American, note the following:

$1.80	'one dollar and eighty cents' *or*
	'one eighty' *or*
	'a dollar eighty'
$2.80	'two dollars and eighty cents' *or*
	'two eighty'

You *cannot* say 'two dollars eighty', 'three dollars seventy-five', etc. Nor can you say 'one dollar eighty'.

The term 'buck' is slang for 'dollar' (on a par with 'quid'). You can say:

$1.00	'one buck' *or*
	'a buck'
$1.80	'a buck eighty'
$2.00	'two bucks'

You *cannot* say 'one buck eighty' or 'one (two, etc.) buck(s) and eighty cents'.

banks and cheques

Unlike in Europe, foreign cheques cannot be used at American banks to obtain cash, so this section won't be of interest to you unless you are going to stay in the USA long enough to open your own bank account.

If you do open a current account (US: checking account) at a bank, you will encounter what one British journalist has described as 'America's extraordinarily rudimentary banking system'. Most American banks are relatively small concerns and are confined to a particular state, area or city. Some have only one branch. One consequence of this is that it is not usually possible to write a cheque (US: check) for cash except at your own bank unless you have made a previous arrangement or can ask a local person to vouch for you. (You can, of course, make out a cheque to a friend with a local bank account.) If you are travelling around, you will therefore have to do what Americans do and take traveller's cheques (hence, of course, the popularity of traveller's cheques). Things are changing, however, and interstate banking seems likely to become easier in the future.

The American banking system has its compensations, though. American banks in some parts of the country work much longer hours than their European equivalents, and it is frequently possible to find banks open at weekends (or at least on Saturdays) and at night, particularly for simple transactions such as paying in or taking out money. (In other areas, however, banks shut at 2 p.m. — and that's it!). Many banks also have 'drive-up windows' — you just sit in your car while you are doing your business — or even whole ranks of drive-in lanes, where you talk to the cashier through loud-speaker grilles and negotiate cash and cheques via vacuum tubes. This is not as scary as it looks; if you don't panic and take time to read the instructions everything goes very smoothly.

Don't be surprised, either, if banks offer you free gifts or goods at a discount when you open an account or deposit large sums of money. They often do things like this to encourage custom.

Note that a 'savings and loans' bank is like a cross between a British savings bank and a building society.

Paying for things by cheque is much more difficult in the USA than it is in Europe. Many businesses, especially petrol stations, and some restaurants simply will not take cheques at all — you will see notices proclaiming 'NO CHECKS'. It is also quite difficult to use cheques in states other than the one in which your bank account is located. And even in your own town, producing a cheque is often regarded, to quote the same journalist, as 'a deeply subversive act'. *using your cheque book*

Nevertheless, Americans do use cheques. They normally write them something like this:

$$\text{One hundred twenty-three and } \frac{63}{100} \text{ DOLLARS } \$123.63$$

If you want to endorse a cheque made out to you so that you can pay the money over to someone else, you should write on the back of the cheque: 'Pay to the order of _____' and sign this, using the form of your name that appears on the front of the cheque. Note, however, that you are not supposed to write this

just anywhere on the back of the cheque. For some
reason, you are supposed to write it sideways (not
lengthwise) across the left-hand end. You will see signs
in shops saying 'NO TWO-PARTY CHECKS'. A two-
party cheque is one that has been paid to you by someone else. There is no such thing in the USA as a crossed
cheque.

Many shops provide a useful service: they will let you
write a cheque for, say, $10 or $20 more than the
amount of your purchase and will give you the difference
in cash. If you are known in a shop, they may let you
cash a cheque even if you are not buying anything.

identification   If businesses do let you use a cheque, they will probably
require some 'ID'. This means *identification*. Some banks
issue European-style cheque-guarantee cards, but most
do not, so you will therefore be asked to produce evidence (sometimes several pieces of evidence, but mostly
two) to prove that you are who your cheque books says
you are. Things that you might be asked to produce
include the following.

1   Your driving licence (US: driver's license). A foreign
     driving licence will often do, but businesses are
     particularly interested in your licence number (which
     is hard to find on a British licence — which of those
     numbers is *the* number?), and they prefer licences
     with photographs, which British licences don't have.
     In some areas there is also an increasing, and
     inconvenient, tendency to accept only *local* driving
     licences.
2   Some other form of ID card. Many American colleges
     and some businesses issue ID cards to their students
     or employees, and most Americans carry all sorts
     of ID around with them, often with photographs
     attached. (The whole thing feels uncomfortably
     totalitarian to the uninitiated.)
3   Your passport, if you carry it with you.
4   Credit cards.

You may also be asked for your local address and telephone number (the proportion of people in the USA
without telephones is extremely low) and for your social
security number. Astonishingly enough, most Americans
have a number that they know by heart and must use,
1984-style, in many official transactions. Unless you are

employed in the USA, however, you will not be privileged
to become a number.

American banks are extremely strict about overdrawn   *overdrafts*
accounts — no polite letters informing you that you are
£50 overdrawn and suggesting that you might perhaps
like to do something about it. Even if you overdraw by
a few dollars, the bank may bounce your cheque. (Because
of this practice, many shops display signs saying things
like '$5 charge for returned checks'.) Even if they don't
bounce your cheque, the bank will certainly charge you
several dollars for their kindness in honouring it.

Geography, Climate and other Natural Hazards

the basics One thing you'll need to know about before leaving home is American weather. Before we discuss this, though, we need to outline the terms people use to describe the different regions of the USA and do some elementary geography. Most often, in America as elsewhere, the regional terms people employ are rather vague and overlapping labels, like 'the Midlands' or 'East Anglia' (is Worcestershire in the Midlands or not?), and people's perceptions of the limits of particular regions depend very much on where they themselves are from. Here are some of the terms you're most likely to come across:

New England	Maine, New Hampshire, Vermont, Massachusetts, Rhode Island, Connecticut.
The Northeast	New England, plus New York, New Jersey, at least part of Pennsylvania, Delaware, Maryland, Washington DC (and the Midwest, for people who live in the West).
The Deep South	Georgia, Alabama, Mississippi; possibly Louisiana, South Carolina, northern Florida.
The South	The Deep South, plus North Carolina, Virginia, Texas; often Arkansas, Kentucky, Tennessee, Florida, possibly Missouri, West Virginia, Oklahoma.
The Midwest	Indiana, Illinois, Iowa; usually Michigan, Ohio, Minnesota, Wisconsin; probably Missouri, Kansas; possibly Nebraska.
The Plains States	North Dakota, South Dakota, Nebraska, Kansas; possibly Iowa, Colorado, Oklahoma, Montana, Wyoming.

The Rockies/	Montana, Wyoming, Colorado, Idaho;
Mountain West	often Utah.
The Southwest	Arizona, New Mexico; possibly Nevada, Utah, Texas, southern California.
The West	Montana, Wyoming, Colorado, Idaho, Arizona, New Mexico, Nevada, Utah; possibly California, Oregon, Washington.
The Northwest	Washington, Oregon; possibly Idaho, northern California.
The West Coast/ Far West	California, Oregon, Washington.

As you can see, areas listed under labels that include the word 'west' extend very far east, and the 'South' actually means the states in the south-east of the country.

The Appalachians (*appa-LAY-shuns*) are a range of mountains running from north to south, parallel to the East Coast, mainly through Pennsylvania, West Virginia, eastern Kentucky and eastern Tennessee, but extending into the Carolinas, Georgia, Virginia, Maryland and Ohio.

A number of the states have 'panhandles'. A 'panhandle' is a narrow strip of land protruding from one corner of a state which, on a map, looks like the handle of a pan. The states in question are Texas, Florida, Oklahoma, Nebraska and Idaho.

The city of Washington is generally known as 'Washinton DC' or simply 'DC' to distinguish it from Washington State. Similarly, New York is often called 'New York City' to distinguish it from the State of New York — or else the state is called 'upstate New York' to distinguish it from the city. The 'Big Apple' is a slang term for New York City.

If you don't want to sound too foreign, you might note the pronunciations of some well-known places:

Albuquerque	*ALbakerkie*
Arkansas	*ARkensaw*
Baton Rouge	*Batten ROOZH*
Des Moines	*De MOYN*
Houston	*Hueston*
La Jolla	*La Hoya*
Los Angeles	*Loss Angelus*
Maryland	*Mairal'nd*
Michigan	*Mishigan*

New Orleans	*New ORleeuns/ORluns*
St Louis	*Saynt Lewiss*
Syracuse	*Sirracuse*
Tucson	*Tooson*
Yosemite	*YaSEMMity*

You may also come across familiar names that are pronounced in unfamiliar ways, such as:

Cairo (Illinois)	*KAYroe*
Peru (Indiana)	*PEEroo*

time zones It is a very long way from the West Coast to the East Coast of America — New York—San Francisco, 2500 miles (4023 kilometres), New York—London 3500 miles (5632 kilometres) — and, as a consequence, the country is divided into four time zones. The Eastern time zone includes places like Boston, New York, Washington, Miami and Cleveland, and is five hours behind British time (i.e. if it is 11 a.m. in London, it is 6 a.m. in New York), except in March—April, when it is six hours behind, since the USA goes on to Summer Time (US: Daylight Saving Time) a few weeks later than Britain. The other American time zones, going from east to west, are Central (including Chicago and New Orleans), Mountain (including Denver and Phoenix) and Pacific (including San Francisco and Seattle). So when it is midday in New York it is 11 a.m. in Chicago, 10 a.m. in Denver and 9 a.m. in San Francisco. Confusingly enough, the boundaries of the time zones do not always coincide with state boundaries (the states bisected by zone lines are Kentucky, Tennessee, North and South Dakota, Nebraska, Kansas, Oregon, Texas, Idaho and Indiana). To make things even more confusing, there are some parts of some states (notably Indiana and Arizona) which do not go on to Daylight Saving Time in the summer, though the vast majority of areas do. If you are driving from one time zone into another, you will sometimes see this indicated on the side of the road — and sometimes not.

The only real problem with the different time zones are remembering about them if you are telephoning someone in a different part of the country; noting that bus and plane timetables always give local times (and, incidentally, use *not* the twenty-four-hour clock system but a.m. and p.m., often abbreviated to 'A' and 'P'); and

remembering that a TV programme that is on at 7 p.m.
in one state may be on at 8 p.m. in the next (though
there is much less of this than you might suppose, since
most programmes, including the news, are recorded and
transmitted later in the more westerly areas).

Most of the USA has a continental climate, with far **weather**
greater extremes than most Western Europeans are used
to. It can get as hot as 110 °F (43 °C) and as cold as
–40 °F. (–40 °C). Many places have extremely cold
winters, or extremely hot summers, or both. And there
are also special American weather hazards. In the late
summer and early autumn hurricanes may strike, particularly along southern parts of the east coast and the
Gulf of Mexico coast. Intensely destructive tornadoes
occur, mainly from mid-April to June, between the
Rockies and the Appalachians. Earthquakes take place
from time to time, especially in California. Forest fires
occur in late summer. And there are torrential and
very noisy thunderstorms — 1500 people are injured by
lightning every year — leading to floods and mudslides
in some areas.

If you're going to America in the summer, you can *summer*
expect northern European-type weather only in the
Pacific Northwest and perhaps in northern areas such as
northern Wisconsin and Maine. Elsewhere, unless you're
in high mountains, it will be much warmer. The southwest
will generally be extremely hot, especially in the desert
areas, and in the rest of the country it can be very hot
indeed. California and the Southwest are generally dry,
while in the Midwest, on the East Coast and in the South
it will often be very humid. In the Midwest especially,
too, it may often be grey, dull and overcast but *very*
hot and humid — don't be misled by just looking out of
the window.
    Most hotels, motels, offices and middle-class homes
in these areas have air-conditioning and, if they don't,
you'll wish they did. Note, however, that air-conditioning
can be very fierce, and you may be glad of a pullover or
a cardigan in restaurants or cinemas.
    Out of doors you can get *very uncomfortable* in hot
and sweaty clothing. Cotton is a good idea, as are short-
sleeved shirts and blouses, sandals and shorts. (Some
older Americans still wear those long Bermuda shorts

that American tourists used to be ridiculous in and famous for, but there's no need for you to.) Be prepared, too, for colossal thunderstorms with very heavy rain.

winter If you are going to America in the winter you can expect British-type weather in the North-west and in parts of the South. In northern California it is generally mild and wet, and southern California and the Southwest are warm-ish. Southern Florida can be very warm. Elsewhere it will range from cold to extremely cold. In the Plains, the Midwest and the Northeast it is quite normal for the temperature to stay below freezing for weeks at a time, and temperatures below 0 °F (−18 °C) are not at all unusual. And you can easily be misled by appearances in the winter too: it can be sunny, with blue skies, and *very* cold.

Snow, ice, ice storms and blizzards are not at all un-common, and these may mean closed airports and blocked or dangerous roads. Drivers may note, however, that temperatures around freezing are often a lot more dangerous than lower temperatures. When it is very cold, it is often very dry − so dry that many people have humidifiers in their homes (see page 95) − and the roads are therefore not icy. Snow ploughs usually do a good job of clearing away snow, but they are powerless against snow blown by the wind and against ice. Salt and sand cannot work either if they are blown off the road by the wind, and salt does not, in any case, work at tempera-tures below 18 °F (−8 °C).

Warm clothing is, obviously, essential for winter visits to the colder parts of the USA, and items such as down-filled jackets and long underwear can be readily found in American stores as well as in department stores and camping shops in Europe. It is also a very good idea to take warm shoes with soles suitable for walking on ice. And do beware of ice on pavements − it is often a lot more slippery than it looks. If you can, walk on snow rather than ice. And if you have to walk on ice, take small steps (or slide your feet along); walk slightly pigeon-toed; put your feet down flat rather than heel-and-toe; and, if you're going to fall over, fall forwards.

spring and autumn In many areas of the USA these are the nicest times of the year, and the autumn in New England is, of course, famous for its beauty. In the Midwest these seasons may

be very short: it's not unknown for it to be below freezing one week and 70 °F (21 °C) the next. But, if you are
lucky, in much of the USA you will find clear, sunny,
warm days with low humidity. If you are unlucky, it will
rain. Tornadoes are especially a spring and early summer
problem, and they really are dangerous. You will be very
unlucky if you actually encounter one (most Americans
have never seen one), but every year several people (at
least) are killed by tornadoes and much property des-
troyed. If you see a tornado when driving, the usual
advice Americans give is to get out of your car and lie in
a ditch, preferably one running at right-angles to the line
of travel of the tornado, stay away from trees (and anything else that can fall on top of you) and protect your
head. If you hear a warning (see below) that a tornado is
coming your way when you are indoors, you should go
to a basement if possible, stay away from windows and
anything that can fall on you (perhaps by sheltering
under a table or mattress) and open windows to prevent
them from imploding. Some towns have tornado shelters.
Tornadoes are typically associated with thunderstorms
and a weird, green-looking sky.

Television stations give detailed and helpful weather **weather**
reports and forecasts, although some forecasters do try **forecasts**
to be perhaps a little too entertaining rather than informative. Radio stations give very frequent temperature
reports and weather forecasts. Note that they often use
the term 'precipitation' (or 'precip.') to refer to rain and
snow. Note too that 'hail' in the USA may refer to
precipitation in which the hail stones are very large
indeed, and that what Americans call 'sleet' may be
rather more hail-like than the more typically slushy
British sleet.

   Forecasts are full of statistics, and tend to say things
like 'There is a 30 per cent chance of precipitation.' The
National Weather Service issues 'tornado watches',
'severe thunderstorm watches' and 'winter storm (i.e.,
blizzard) watches' if weather of these types is threatened,
and these are broadcast by radio and TV stations. If a
tornado or storm is definitely on the way, then the
'watch' becomes a 'warning'. 'Travellers' advisories' are
also issued if road conditions are likely to be bad because
of snow, ice, wind or fog.

   In the colder areas of the country in winter reports

and forecasts also give what is referred to as 'wind-chill'. The actual air temperature may not be very informative if it is windy, because the effect of cold on the body and the chance of frostbite may be greatly increased by the speed of the wind. Thus the actual temperature may be 20 °F (-7 °C) but with wind-chill the effect on the body might be that of a temperature of -10 °F (-23 °C). Americans will then say 'The wind-chill (or wind-chill factor) is -10 °; but this actually means that the temperature including the wind-chill factor is equivalent to -10 °. It is not unknown for the wind-chill to drop to as low as -60 °F (-51 °C), in which case people are recommended to stay at home.

Some TV and radio stations include, in addition to things like pollution indexes and record high and low temperatures, measurements of 'heating degree days' (in winter) and 'cooling degree days' (in summer). A 'degree day' is the number of degrees by which the average temperature on a given day has deviated from 65 °F (18 °C), and the seasonal 'degree days index' is the sum of the 'degree days' for that season. The cumulative index thus gives an indication of, say, how severe a winter it has been and of heating costs by comparison with those of previous winters.

flora and fauna to watch out for

America is a rather more dangerous place to live in than Europe — and not just because it is inhabited by Americans (see the section on violence and safety, page 82). We have already noted the inimical climate; when this is combined with some of the hostile flora and fauna with which America abounds, it makes one think that the country may not really be suitable for human habitation at all.

There are, of course, exotically dangerous animals like snakes, which can occasionally be encountered in fields, woods, rivers and lakes, as well as in the deserts and mountains. (They are not all dangerous, but some are.) And there are grizzly bears, which you will not meet unless you venture into the mountains, and black and brown bears, which are more common (you can come across them in some of the remoter forests) but less agressive. If you want to make sure that you don't meet a bear, make a lot of noise as you walk. And if you are camping overnight, take local advice, particularly on how to store food.

A much more common hazard is the insects. In many parts of the country people defend their homes against insects with screens and regular visits from pest-control agencies (see page 98). Houses can be infested by ants, termites and cockroaches, and in addition to being stung by wasps, hornets and bees, you run the risk of being bitten by mosquitoes and spiders. Most spider bites are rater like mosquito bites; in most parts of the country spiders are not poisonous. There are poisonous spiders (black widows) in the Southwest, however.

Raccoons, opossums and other wild animals may look friendly, if you happen to see them, but can be vicious if frightened — so be careful. Skunks, of course, are not dangerous, but they do emit a very bad smell. You are most likely to encounter this smell when driving. Skunks often seem to get themselves run over (you will see small black-and-white carcasses at the side of the road), and unfortunately their smell lingers on after them. If you are unlucky enough to be sprayed by a skunk, the best thing to do, apparently, is burn your clothes (there is no way you can remove the smell by washing) and wash your hair in tomato juice!

In the swamplands of the South you may encounter alligators. Alligators are not dangerous unless provoked.

Some parts of the American coast are troubled by sharks. If you can't see anyone swimming, ask the locals if it is OK to do so.

America also has some dangerous plants, notably poison ivy, poison oak and poison sumac. If you're out in the woods, don't touch or sit on anything unless you're sure of what it is. These plants bring you out in an unpleasant, spreading rash, which may require a visit to the doctor. Poison ivy looks a little like Virginia creeper, but its leaves grow in groups of three. The leaves are green and shiny except in the spring and autumn, when they turn a reddish colour.

Don't let any of the above worry you. Most of the 225 million Americans get through each year without sustaining too much damage, and you'll probably manage it too.

Making Telephone Calls

The American telephone system is really excellent and compares very favourably indeed with the British system. Lines are always clear; calls nearly always go through; and if you want a phone installed, you can get one *instantly*. The Post Office has nothing to do with the telephone system in the USA, and the network is run by private companies. (These compete for long-distance customers, and if you acquire your own phone you may have a bewildering series of decisions to make about which company to go with. The *easiest* thing to do is to just stick with AT&T, the company that owns the phone lines and handles local calls.)

One of the first things you may have to do when you arrive in the USA is to make a phone call, perhaps from a public call box (US: phone booth, pay phone). If you take your time and read the instructions, this is easy enough. Full details of rates and methods of making calls are given in telephone directories, but you may find the following points useful.

dialling, ringing and engaged tones

The dialling tone is a continuous hum. In many areas it is necessary to insert coins into a pay phone, as for a local call (see below), in order to get a dialling tone. The ringing tone is normally a longish, repeated, single ring. The engaged (US: busy) signal is a faster, repeated beep.

If you call an airline or a business in Britain, you very frequently get the engaged signal, or else the phone rings for ages before someone answers. American concerns, particularly those with toll-free numbers (see below), often have a much better system than this. First, you get a recording that tells you that all personnel are busy and asks you to hold on. Then you listen to a recording of soft music, designed to calm you down while you wait, and when someone eventually answers, they say nice things, like 'Thank you for your patience.' It would be nice, wouldn't it, if British businesses thought of doing something similar?

American telephone numbers are normally in the form (123) 456-7890. (In some cities an older system, replacing some of the figures with letters, is still in use.) The three figures in brackets constitute the 'area code', which corresponds to the British Subscriber Trunk Dialling (STD) code. Note, though, that the areas covered by American area codes are normally much larger than those covered by STD codes. The principle, however, is the same: if you are calling a number within the same area (i.e. with the same area-code prefix), you do not dial the area code; if you are calling a number with a different area code, you do dial it.

codes

A call to a number in the same city or immediate locality (check the directory for maps if necessary) is a local call.

local calls

If you are ringing from a private phone, the call is free in most places — which means that it is not *particularly* rude to pick up the phone in someone else's house and make a local call. (If you know the people well enough to use their toilet without asking, you can probably do the same with their phone, though it would be more usual to tell them you'd like to use the phone.)

If you are ringing from a pay phone you will, obviously, have to pay. You simply insert the coins before dialling. In most places the cost for a local call is usually 25 cents. If the latter, you can insert four nickels, two dimes, a combination of nickels and dimes — or a quarter, in which case you waste five cents, since you get no change.

Dial 0. You may have to insert coins to obtain a dialling tone first (see above). If there is no charge for the call, your coins will be returned by the machine.

calling the operator

Any call outside your immediate vicinity is a long-distance call, regardless of whether it is within the same area code or not, though the greater the distance, the higher the cost usually — in some cases in-state calls are more expensive than out-of-state calls.

long-distance calls

In very many places for a long-distance call you have to dial 1 before you start dialling the number you want (complete with area code if it is different from that of the phone you are calling from). In other places the 1 is not necessary, and you simply dial the area code and number. If in doubt, dial 1 anyway — if it is unnecessary, the dialling tone will continue, and you just dial the remaining numbers.

If you are ringing from a call box, the procedure is the same, except that you may have to press a button to select a particular phone company — it doesn't seem to matter which you select. After you have dialled, the operator will cut in and tell you how much money to put in for the first three minutes. You cannot pay for less — quick ten-second calls of the British STD type are not possible. It is a good idea to have a supply of quarters, dimes and nickels available (no other coins can be used), as long-distance calls are surprisingly expensive.

After the three minutes the operator will cut in again and ask you to put in more money for additional minutes. Sometimes he or she will wait until after you have completed the call and then ask you to put in extra — sometimes even by ringing the phone after you have replaced it. There is, of course, no way the operator can *make* you insert more coins or pick up the ringing phone, but if you don't, the call will be charged to the number you phoned!

It is possible to make long-distance calls by simply dialling 0 and asking the operator to connect you, but generally they prefer you to dial the call yourself, even though when you do, you will have to talk to the operator anyway.

There are, as in other countries, different rates for long-distance calls at different times of day, and peak rates can be three times as high as the low rates.

reversing the charges A transfer-charge or reversed-charge call is known in the USA as a 'collect' call. (You will not normally want to make a local call collect, but if you don't have any coins and therefore need to, and if you are in an area where coins are not necessary to get a dialling tone, dial 0 and tell the operator you want to make a collect local call.) If you want to make a long-distance call collect, you proceed as described above for long-distance calls, except that you dial 0 before dialling the area code (where appropriate) and number. (In areas where it is necessary to dial 1 for long-distance calls, the 0 *replaces* the 1.) Operators then cut in and ask if they can help you. You tell them you want to make this a collect call, and they will then want to know your name (your first name will often do) and, sometimes, the number you're dialling from. They sometimes, too, want an assurance that the number you're calling is not a call box.

Collect calls are much more expensive than ordinary calls.

It is also possible to make 'person-to-person' calls, for which you will not be charged unless a particular person specified by you is unavailable to talk to you. For a person-to-person call proceed as for a collect call.

person-to-person calls

Person-to-person calls also cost a lot more than ordinary calls.

In many parts of the USA, you can dial direct to Europe. For example, you dial 011 to get an international line, 44 for the UK, the STD code *without* the 0, and then the number. Thus to call the Edinburgh number (031) 123-4567 you dial 011-44-31-123-4567. It doesn't always work at first. If it doesn't keep trying. And it can take a *long* time for the connection to go through — maybe twenty seconds.

international calls

If you can't dial direct from where you are, you will have to dial 0 and go through the operator. (Don't be surprised if, before asking if he or she can help you, the operator says something incomprehensible — this will be his or her first name. In some areas the phone companies are encouraging operators to introduce themselves in order to foster an image of friendliness.)

It often saves time to tell the operator that the code for the UK, for example, is 44, to tell him that the city code (this is what they call British STD codes) that you want is such-and-such — you should give the number *without* the prefix 0 — and then tell him the number you want to call.

Normally, making any call through the operator is much more expensive than dialling direct. However, if you make an international call through the operator because direct dialling is not available, you will be charged at the lower rate.

You will have observed that in order to make an international direct-dial call, you start by dialling 011, which begins with 0. An intelligent question would be: 'Why doesn't this just get you the operator, since to get the operator you also dial 0?' The answer seems to be that there is a delay that operates after you dial 0 to see if you are going to dial anything else before the operator is alerted. In other words, if you're dialling 011, don't hesitate after the 0.

phoning from hotels and motels

In some hotels and motels you will have to go through the hotel switchboard to make a call from your room. Very often, though, you will be able to dial direct. You may have to dial one number (perhaps 9) to get an outside line for a local call, and a different number (perhaps 8) to get a line for a long-distance or international call. If you dial a long-distance or international call, an operator may cut in and ask you for your room or extension number (and the cost of your call will, of course, be placed on your room bill).

toll-free numbers

A number of businesses and other concerns, including airline offices, have what are called 'toll-free' numbers with an 800 prefix. This means that you can call them from a private or pay phone without it costing you anything. Note that if you are in an area where 1 has to be dialled for a long-distance call, the 1 must be dialled before the 800.

emergencies

There is no nationwide 999-type emergency system. There are emergency numbers that you can call, and these are sometimes indicated on pay phones, but they vary from place to place. The easiest thing to do if in a panic is to ring the operator (by dialling 0 or pressing the button labelled 'operator'), though the operator may take a long time to answer. This situation may change, as attempts are being made to institute a national system.

If you are in an area where it is necessary to insert coins into a pay phone in order to get a dialling tone and you don't have any change, you're in trouble.

making yourself understood

Americans do not normally say 'double two', 'double three', etc. If the number you want is 33699 and you are making the call via the operator, say 'three-three-six-nine-nine' or perhaps 'thirty-three, six, ninety-nine'.

Similarly, if you have to spell out names, note that most (particularly younger) Americans are unfamiliar with the convention of saying, for example, 'double R' or 'double L' (which will generally be interpreted as 'W'). Any name that contains a doubled letter (for instance, Mann) should be spelled out in full: say 'M-A-N-N' rather than 'M-A-double N'.

The operator may ask you if your call is a 'station' call. This is short for 'station-to-station' and simply means an ordinary call — you are willing to speak to whoever answers the phone — as opposed to a person-to-person call.

Do not ask the operator if you are 'through' yet. To Americans 'through' means 'done', 'finished', 'over', and they will find the question puzzling. ('How should I know?') Instead you should ask if you are 'connected'.

private phones

If you are in the USA long enough to acquire your own phone, you will find that a number of services are available in America that are currently not available in the UK — and you will soon wish they were. Bills are payable monthly, but they come complete with a printout of all your long-distance calls. (This may make adulterous phone calls inadvisable, but is in every other way an advantage.) It is also possible to charge to your own number a call you make from someone else's phone by telling the operator you want to charge the call to a 'third number'. (It is sometimes even possible to do this from a pay phone, especially if there is someone by your own phone to confirm with the operator that this is OK.) It is also possible, for not much extra cost, to obtain facilities for forwarding calls automatically to another number while you are out, and for holding calls that come in while you are talking to someone else — a really convenient service.

Hiring and Driving a Car

One of the best ways to get around the USA is by car; depending on how long you intend to stay, you may want to borrow, hire, lease or even buy one. (If the latter, note that in America cars cost about 50 per cent of what they cost in the UK.)

Americans have the reputations of being good and careful drivers. This is not unjustified. Americans are generally very used to cars. And road conditions (with straight, wide, relatively uncrowded roads), large, comfortable cars, an overall top speed limit of 55 miles (88.5 kilometres) per hour and vigilant police all combine to make for a comparatively relaxed and civilized driving style. This does not mean, however, that you will not find aggressive driving in some of the bigger cities. And you will also encounter many careless drivers who do not signal what they are going to do until after they have done it, if at all, and crazy drivers who pull out in front of you without looking. And (particularly in the Mid-west, West and South) there are young men around who seem to be attempting to prove their masculinity by carving up everybody else on the road, including foreign tourists. Driving is perhaps at its best on the East and West Coasts.

hiring a car In the USA this is referred to as 'renting' a car and is generally cheaper than in Europe. It is also a very common thing for Americans to do, particularly when travelling away from home, because of the low level of public transport provision. You can find car rental desks at airports, and when travelling by air it is a good idea at busy periods to ring ahead of you and reserve a rental car so that you can be sure that one of the type you want is available when you arrive. Information on toll-free numbers to call to make reservations, and on other rental offices, can be obtained from hotels and from the telephone book Yellow Pages.

Note that, surprisingly enough, some car rental companies *will not accept cash* — you need a credit card.

(They can then trace you if you've stolen or damaged the car.)

It is very often possible to get a 'one-way rental': you hire a car in one place and leave it in another. This can be extremely convenient, although it is normally much more expensive. All sorts of other deals are also often available. Prices may vary according to what time of the week it is, as well as whether mileage is included or not. It is worthwhile checking around different firms to see which has the best arrangement for your particular plans.

In many towns there are offices, completely separate from rental firms, from which you can obtain cars to drive to other cities *free of charge*, except that you have to pay for (at least some of) your own petrol. You will also have to leave and arrive on specified dates. The cars themselves normally belong to people who are moving house or to businesses that need cars transferred for some reason. You get to deliver the car for them — and a free ride. Look in the telephone book under 'Drive-Away Cars'.

American cars are generally much larger and heavier than European and Japanese cars, although there is now a big increase in the production of smaller cars.   **choosing your car**

The larger cars are extremely comfortable and relaxing

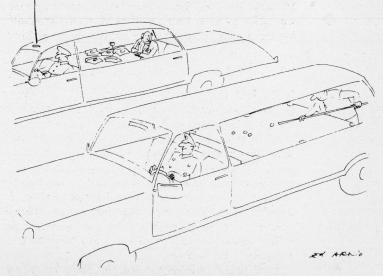

Drawing by Ed Arno; © 1984 The New Yorker Magazine, Inc.

to drive and be driven in, but they do not generally handle or corner as well as smaller cars. They also consume colossal amounts of petrol, although there has been a big improvement in this respect in recent years, and 'economy' cars are taking over from 'gas-guzzlers'.

You may well encounter gadgets in American cars that you have not had the pleasure of coming across before. These include electric windows and mirrors, and buzzers that tell you that your seat belt is not fastened, that you've left your lights on, that you've left the keys in the ignition, etc. Your car may be equipped with 'cruise control', a device that enables you to free your right foot on long motorway trips (it will keep the car going at a constant speed until you accelerate or brake) and air-conditioning (very desirable, though not as absolutely necessary as Americans may tell you for desert and other hot driving). Cars with air-conditioning are sometimes said to 'have air'.

You will be able to select a car from among the following types:

sedan	saloon
station wagon	estate
compact	medium, European-sized car
sub-compact	something of the size of, for example, a VW Golf (called a Rabbit in the USA).

For larger American cars terms such as 'economy', mid-size' and 'luxury' are used.

If you are at all anxious about changing gear with the 'wrong' hand — if you are used to driving on the left — it is a good idea to choose an automatic, even if you are more familiar with a gear lever. It takes almost no time to adapt to automatic transmission.

car insurance   In some parts of the USA, astonishingly enough, it is *not* compulsory to have third-party car insurance. You may therefore be run into by someone who damages or wrecks your car and maims or injures you *and is not insured*. Many American motorists take out 'uninsured motorist insurance'. If you are hiring a car in the USA, you may want to take out personal accident insurance before you leave home — and let the rental company worry about the car.

useful   You probably already know about most of the differences
vocabulary   between British and American car terminology, but in

case you don't, these are some terms you may come
across:

hood	bonnet
trunk	boot
muffler	silencer
windshield	windscreen
spark plug	sparking plug
carburetor	carburettor
tire	tyre
flat	puncture

(See also *pavement*, p. 132)

In American English shock absorbers are known colloquially as 'shocks', whereas in Britain they are often called
'shockers'. Americans often talk of a car's 'pick-up', while
Britons would speak of 'acceleration'. Americans also
talk about 'changing a tire' when the British would say
'changing a wheel'. 'Changing a tire' is what Americans
do when they have a 'flat', and they do *not* mean taking
the tyre off the rim of the wheel and putting on another.

Datsun is generally pronounced *Dahtsun*, Nissan is
Nee-sarn, and Renault is often pronounced *Re-NAWLT*.

American roads

In some respects American roads are a good deal better
than most European roads. They are, for instance,
generally much wider and straighter. In other respects
they are worse. The combination of low taxes and (in
the north) severe frosts means that even motorways may
have amazing pot-holes. There are also, generally speaking, fewer road markings, cats' eyes and so on than
Europeans are used to.

driving on the right: hints for 'left-side' drivers

It is not driving on the wrong side of the road that is the
hardest thing about driving in the USA for the British,
Australian, Japanese and others: as any British driver
who has driven in Europe will know, after the first five
minutes this is not very difficult. The hardest thing about
driving in America is driving on the wrong side of the
car. You have to remember that the mirror, hand brake
and gear lever are all on your right, and that you should
look over your right shoulder when reversing.

Most difficult of all, though, is judging your distance
from the edge of the road on your right. Years of experience at doing this on your left doesn't seem to help, and

it's rather like learning to drive all over again as far as
this particular point is concerned. However, it is not *very*
difficult, and it doesn't take long to master, particularly
if you have a passenger with you to help you to keep
your distance from the kerb.

Driving an automatic (as you probably will be if you
are hiring a car) removes the problem of changing gear
with your right hand (or, as often happens in an emergency, with the window winder).

rules of the road Driving rules and customs vary in detail from state to
state, but there are some general respects in which they
differ from those in Europe.

speed The overall top speed limit is 55 miles (88.5 kilometres)
per hour. This is fairly rigidly enforced in many areas.
If you really feel that you want to go faster, see what
other drivers are doing, particularly those with 'CBs'.
These are Citizen Band radios, and you can identify cars
that have them by the additional, larger-than-usual aerials
placed on the back. Owners of CBs keep in touch with
each other and report on the location of police cars (as
well as on accidents, breakdowns, etc.). Lorries frequently
have CBs.

traffic lights American traffic lights go green—amber—red—green. In
other words, there is no red-and-amber phase before the
green. This means that you may be caught napping at
what you thought was still a red light unless you keep
your wits about you.

Nearly everywhere in the USA (the main exception is
Manhattan, New York City) it is possible, unless
indicated to the contrary, to turn right on a red light,
provided that you stop first and give way, of course, to
oncoming traffic. (That is, you treat the red light as a
stop sign.) You must also give way to pedestrians crossing
at the lights. Busy intersections often have signs indicating that turning on a red light is *not* allowed (sometimes only at certain times of day).

One wonders why this very sensible system has not
been introduced into Europe — although it has been
claimed in the USA that this rule has led to an increase
in accidents.

U-turns U-turns are *not allowed* in 'business districts' — i.e.,
town centres — unless specifically indicated.

American practice when turning at a crossroads is different from that in Britain. If two cars approach an inter-
section from opposite directions and both want to turn
left, *they pass in front of each other* rather than behind.
You have to watch carefully for cars coming towards
you and going straight ahead.

*turning at
crossroads*

Probably the biggest difference between European and
American driving practice is that on motorways and other
roads with more than one lane in each direction, it is
perfectly normal for American drivers to pass other cars
on the inside (i.e., on the right), which is, of course, a
serious offence in Britain and some other European
countries. (Australians, however, will find it quite
normal.)

overtaking

This is very disconcerting at first, particularly if you're
in the middle lane and are being passed on both sides at
once by large lorries. It also means that you *must* check
to your right before moving into an inside lane. Most
Americans, in fact, look over their right shoulder before
performing this manoeuvre, because even if they have a
wing or door mirror, the larger cars are so large that there
is a considerable blind spot. Although slower traffic is
supposed to keep to the right, there is a strong tendency
in the USA, as a result of this way of driving, for drivers
to get into one lane and stay there — a practice known as
'lane driving'. (This is on the part of the sensible driver.
On the part of the non-sensible driver there is a strong
tendency to weave in and out from one lane to another.)

Technically speaking, it is legal to 'go past' another
vehicle on the right but not to 'pass'. The difference
between these two is that in 'going past' you are already
in the right lane and stay there, whereas in 'passing' you
are in the same lane as the vehicle to be overtaken and
move to your right in order to overtake it, subsequently
pulling back into your original lane. One does, nevertheless, observe lots of illegal 'passing' going on. Slow-moving
traffic is supposed to stay in the right-hand lane.

Americans do not talk about 'headlights' vs. 'dipped
headlights'. Instead they talk of 'brights' vs. 'headlights'.

*headlights,
sidelights and
the indicator*

Driving with sidelights only (US: parking lights) is not
permitted.

Note that on many American cars there is no separate
rear indicator light — the rear light simply flashes on and

off. Thus a flashing red light is probably an indicator and *not* a sign that the brakes are being applied repeatedly.

school buses Because of the inadequacy of public transport systems in the USA, most areas have special school buses (which take children to and from school once a day, five days a week, and do nothing at all for most of the rest of the time). These are usually painted yellow. When they stop to discharge children they display flashing red lights, and it is then illegal to pass the bus, even if you are going in the opposite direction on the other side of the road. All traffic must stop.

the police If a policeman in a police car wants you to stop, he will not overtake you and stop you from in front. Instead he will drive along behind you flashing his overhead lights, which are usually red (sometimes yellow or blue). Once you have stopped, some Americans recommend that you stay in your car and let the policeman come to you.

Keep your hands visible, and don't do anything (such as lunging for the glove compartment) that might look as if you were going for a gun.

Have your driving licence ready — it will be the first thing that the policeman asks for. Americans are very puzzled by British driving licences, especially by the lack of a photograph. An International Driving Licence, which does have a photograph, can help, but is not actually necessary for visitors.

road signs If you can read English, you can normally understand American road signs. There are relatively few European-style iconic signs.

Direction signs normally have a green background. PED XING is not Chinese. It means 'pedestrian crossing'.

no entry In place of the European no-entry sign, Americans put up signs saying 'NO ENTRY'. Motorways have very nice no-entry signs saying things like 'GO BACK' and 'WRONG WAY'.

one way One-way streets in towns are not always very well pro-

vided with no-entry signs. You have to be alert for small
road signs with an arrow on a black background bearing
the words 'ONE WAY'.

Stop signs are red and octagonal. On American signs
'YIELD' means 'give way'.

'stop' and
'give way'

The USA has very few roundabouts. It does, though,
have an institution known as the 'four-way stop'. As you
approach a crossroads, you may see a stop sign with the
words '4 WAY' underneath. This means that all four of
the roads involved have stop signs on them. Priority goes
to the vehicle that has arrived and stopped at the crossroads first. If two drivers stop at exactly the same time,
a driver supposedly gives way to the vehicle on his right.
(This ought to mean that if four vehicles stop at a crossroads at precisely the same time, they would all have to
stay there indefinitely, but this does not seem to happen
in practice.)

Crossroads are not as well provided with white lines
and other markings as they are in Europe. As one does
from time to time encounter crossroads with no indication at all of priority, it is sometimes difficult to know,
even if you think you are on a main road, whether you
have right of way or not. What you have to do in this case
is to see if the other road has a stop sign. The octagonal
shape is very distinctive, and you can tell even from the
back that it is a stop sign.

At night, traffic lights at some junctions are switched
so that they flash. A flashing red light functions as a stop
sign, while a flashing amber light means 'You have
priority; proceed with care.'

Bus lanes are often indicated by diamond symbols
painted on the road. There may be no other clear
indication that that is what they are.

bus lanes

There seem to be more parking restrictions in the USA
than there are in Europe. Most Americans appear to get
parking tickets. If you get one and feel like paying it, in
many places the system is that an envelope is left on
your car so that you can post your fine to the appropriate
place. Some states swap parking-ticket information, while
others don't. If your parking ticket is issued in a state a
long way from the one in which your car is registered,
you probably need not bother to pay it.

parking

© M. Stevens.

You must *not* park in front of a fire-hydrant. It is important to remember this because there will be no signs anywhere to tell you. Fire-hydrants are easily recognized: they are large metal kerbside objects, perhaps two feet high, with parking spaces in front of them.

You *must* park in the direction of traffic flow, even in the daytime. Combined with the no U-turns rule, this means that there is no way you can get to a parking space on the other side of the road unless you go round the block and come back.

'Head-in' parking means that you must drive into the parking space frontwards.

Parking meters mostly take quarters, dimes and nickels, but there are some that take pennies.

At some urban car parks (US: parking lots) you have to leave your car keys with an attendant and he parks your car for you. A similar system, known as 'valet parking', is also used at the more expensive hotels and restaurants.

Some streets in the northern part of the country are designated and labelled 'snow streets'. You must not leave your car on these streets if snowfall exceeds a certain amount (specified on the sign). This restriction is, of course, designed to permit snow ploughs to clear the street. If you *do* leave your car illegally on a 'snow street', it will be towed away.

Some streets and other areas are labelled 'tow-away zone'. This means that if you park illegally in these areas, your car will be towed away (and it will too). You'll have to pay to get it back — and it won't be cheap.

The American motorway (US: freeway) system is very extensive, and you will almost certainly find yourself using it if you are driving any distance at all. Many motorways have only two lanes in each direction, although in urban and other busy areas you may encounter as many as eight lanes. Motorways are badly cleared and maintained: the surface may be very rough, and the hard shoulder (US: shoulder or 'berm') may be littered with stripped tyres and other debris. The central reservation of a motorway is called the 'median'. Slip roads are called 'ramps'.

motorway driving

On motorways there is a *minimum* speed limit as well as a maximum. This minimum speed limit is 40 miles (64 kilometres) per hour, unless otherwise indicated. If car trouble or bad weather forces you to drive more slowly than this, you should switch on your hazard-warning lights.

speed

The interstate highway system uses even numbers for east—west roads and odd numbers for north—south roads (the I-80 goes from New York to San Francisco, for example, and the I-55 from Chicago to New Orleans). Three-figure numbers usually denote urban ringroad motorways or other minor motorways. Direction signs most often show the number of the road and its direction (north, south etc.), *not* its destination. Note that JCT means 'junction'.

the road-numbering system

Motorways do not normally have emergency telephones. If you break down, you have to wait for the police, the highway patrol — or someone with a CB.

Motorways may be provided with rest areas and toilets (of very variable quality). They do not, however, normally have other facilities. If you want petrol or food, you will

motorway facilities

have to leave the motorway. Petrol stations and restaurants are, however, normally close to exits and are well indicated and signposted.

toll roads A number of motorways are toll roads. These are often better quality than the others and do have service areas (US: oases) with petrol stations and restaurants actually on the motorway. In urban areas you pay the toll, if you have the right change, by dropping your money into a basket. In other areas you may be given a ticket as you join the motorway and pay a human being when you leave.

motorway Watch out for 'exit only' lanes. Driving in the inside lane
exits is not always as relaxing as it is in Britain, since before an exit the inside lane may turn into an 'all vehicles must exit' lane, and you therefore have to move over to your left, which is not always easy if there is a lot of traffic.

Be careful not to leave the motorway by mistake. At exits the edge of the road is often unmarked, and you may find yourself following what you think is the edge of the motorway when it is, in fact, the edge of the slip road. The problem is compounded by the fact that there are often no arrows or other signs showing what is going on.

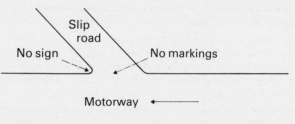

One of the scariest features of American motorways is that they sometimes have exits from the fast lane, particularly in urban areas and at motorway junctions. Often these are not indicated very far ahead, and you may find yourself having to cross several lanes of traffic rapidly in order to leave the motorway.

Another trick designed to confuse foreign visitors at exits is that, quite frequently, the slip road leading onto the motorway is situated *before* the slip road leading off. This can, obviously, be very dangerous.

'Gas stations' (as they are known in the USA) tend, on **garages**
average and particularly in rural areas, to be rather more
dilapidated than they are in Europe. In many gas stations *petrol pumps*
you will notice a distinction between 'self-serve' pumps
and 'full-serve' pumps. In the case of the latter the petrol
is more expensive, but you will get your windscreen
cleaned and, if you choose, your oil checked. Some 'self-
serve' gas stations really are equipped as self-service
establishments. Others are not — they are simply ordinary
petrol stations whose owners have decided to save money
by making them self-service without spending any money
on modifications. This means that the pumps are harder
to operate and that the attendants have no record inside
the station of how much you owe — they either take
your word for it or else come out and have a look,
which rather defeats the object.

Be careful, at self-service stations, not to splash yourself with petrol. Petrol seems to come out faster than in
Europe, and frequently the automatic switch-off device
does not work properly. This is particularly the case at
unmodified 'self-serve' as opposed to self-service stations.

Petrol comes in three main types: unleaded (for newer *petrol*
cars that must, mechanically and by law, run on petrol
with no lead content), regular and super. (Super unleaded
is also available.) Even super is not a very high-octane
fuel by British standards.

Petrol is much cheaper than it is in Europe. People
who are used to reckoning in gallons should bear in mind
that American gallons (and therefore American quarts
and pints) are only five-sixths the volume of British
(Imperial) gallons (see page 136). A car that does 24 miles
to the British gallon will do only 20 miles to the American
gallon. Visitors who are used to buying their petrol in
litres should note that an American gallon is 3.6 litres.

Oil is normally sold in quarts in the USA. One American *oil*
quart is equivalent to 1.6 British pints (0.9 litres).

Gas stations generally have toilets. Some of them are *toilets*
clean, some not. Many gas-station owners and attendants
have no objection to your using their toilets even if you
do not buy anything. Very often the toilets are located
outside, round the side of the building. The ladies' is

often locked — you have to get the key from the attendant. (For more on toilets, see page 81.)

food and drink

Gas stations often sell sweets (US: candy) and other items, and many have vending machines supplying cold soft drinks.

repairs

Watch out at garages for people offering you repairs you do not need (cf. American doctors, page 129). There are reports in the American press of operators who replace worn shock absorbers and faulty exhaust systems that are not worn or faulty, and who even puncture your tyres when you are not looking and then 'notice' a flat tyre so that they can sell you a new one or carry out a repair. This practice is said to be most common in the West, in such states as Nevada, and at garages close to motorway exits. Cars with out-of-state number plates are particularly liable to receive this treatment, apparently.

car washes

In addition to the familiar type of car wash, you may in America come across two other types. In the case of the first, you wash down your own car with hoses, brushes and leathers. With the second, you get out of your car and wait in comfort while real live people take your car through a line, where, in addition to being washed mechanically, it is washed, cleaned and polished by hand, inside and out.

long journeys by car

useful accessories and hints

Take a tyre gauge with you on any long trip. Most gas stations have air lines, but for some reason very few of these have built-in pressure gauges. Attendants may be willing to check your tyre pressure for you, but they are often somewhat slapdash about it, and you may prefer to do it yourself.

If you are not familiar with automatic-transmission cars, remember that on long journeys the transmission fluid should be checked from time to time as well as the oil.

It is obvious if you think about it, but this point may escape you in the heat of the moment: you can't bump-start an automatic car if the battery is flat (US: dead). For this reason many Americans carry 'jumper cables', which they can run from their battery to that of another car. You may feel that you would like to carry one too, but if you don't have one and your battery is flat, you should not find it too difficult to get someone to help you in this way. (Americans call it 'jumping' a car.)

If you are taking a long trip in the summer, it is a very good idea to buy a thermos chest or 'cooler' and to keep your food and drinks in it. You can buy packs of ice at supermarkets and gas stations to keep the cooler cool. If you are driving across deserts, take plenty of water with you, and drive at night if you can.

Note that you are not allowed to drive into Arizona or California if you are carrying any fruit.

It is not too easy to find good, detailed maps of the USA. *maps* There is nothing approaching the Ordnance Survey, for instance (the country, is of course, *much* larger), and the road atlases appear to be designed by morons. You might expect that, like road atlases of Britain or Europe, they would be divided up so that each page covered an area of the same size and so that adjacent pages covered adjacent areas. This does seem the only way to do it. However, Americans have invented another way of doing it, which manages to be both less obvious *and* less intelligent. Most road atlases are divided up *by state*, and the states are arranged *in alphabetical order*. It is not difficult to appreciate that, though the pages are the same size, the different states are not. Some concessions are made to these differences (e.g. Texas might warrant two pages), but the atlases are difficult to use, and the planning of journeys can be a tiresome business. However, the American Automobile Association (AAA or 'Triple A') provides trip maps arranged in geographical order, and good sheet maps can be obtained from gas stations and information offices.

America is a very big country, and distances can be *distances* enormous. Don't be misled, just by looking at a map, into thinking you can go farther than you can — be sure to calculate the mileage involved. (This applies equally to planning bus and plane trips.) On the other hand, in normal conditions and when you are travelling on motorways, you can generally average 50 miles (80 kilometres) per hour at least, and it is perfectly possible to travel 500 miles (800 kilometres) in a day, or even further, if you have the desire and the stamina.

American lorries (US: trucks) can be extremely long and *dangerous and* large. Watch out for side draughts as they go past. *irritating*

The class of vehicle known as a 'recreational vehicle' *vehicles* (RV) includes caravans (US: trailers) and 'motor homes'.

The latter are caravans in which people traverse the country on holiday consuming vast amounts of petrol, slowing down traffic and sometimes even towing small cars or boats behind them. Though they like to think of themselves as nomads, owners of RVs often provide themselves with colour TVs and stay at camping sites complete with plug-in water, sewage and electricity facilities. (RVs can be hired and are excellent for touring around in, though they are not particularly cheap.)

bumper stickers
Americans are bombarded by so much advertising on TV and elsewhere that they are often driven to fight back by advertising themselves. They do this in two ways — by wearing T-shirt slogans, and by placing 'bumper stickers' on their cars. These are the equivalent of the windscreen stickers you see in Europe, but they are placed on the rear bumper — and are much more numerous. They are of considerable anthropological interest and may keep you entertained, if not always amused, on long journeys. Some are political; others range from the suggestive ('Divers do it deeper'), to the religious/nauseating ('Honk if you love Jesus'), to the domestic/nauseating ('Have you hugged your kid today?'), to the insane ('Guns don't cause crime any more than flies cause manure').

winter driving
Driving on frost, ice and snow is obviously more difficult and dangerous than ordinary driving and is necessary much more often in large areas of the USA than it is in Britain (see page 16). Clearly, one has to drive more slowly and more carefully and, in particular, avoid sharp braking, acceleration and lane changing. Automatic cars especially have to be gingerly handled, as it is less easy to use the gears in these cars to slow the vehicle down. On motorways watch out for bridges — these become icy before other parts of the road do.

In mountainous and other snowy areas, chains are used in snowy conditions and can be hired (often at exorbitant prices) if you do not want to buy them. In many states, however, chains — as well as the studded tyres used in Scandinavia, which greatly increase the safety of driving on slippery roads — are, regrettably, not permitted. (They damage road surfaces, of course, though why better summer road surfaces are preferred to fewer winter accidents and injuries is not easy to understand. Perhaps Americans would rather have more accidents than pay more taxes.) Instead, Americans fit 'snow tires' to their rear wheels in winter conditions. These are tyres that have thicker treads and increase traction in snow. They are not, however, any good against ice.

If you are driving in wintry conditions take food and a warm drink with you, and put a shovel in the boot for digging yourself out of snow. It is also a good idea to take something to put under the wheels to give you traction if you are stuck on ice — many Americans take cat litter! Make sure, too, that you have warm clothing, including especially a hat, and a blanket.

Do not underestimate the problems caused by blizzards. Heavy snow blown by strong winds can reduce visibility even more severely than fog.

In bad conditions the police may announce that roads, including motorways, are closed. It is then a serious offence to try and drive on any of these roads — as well as being dangerous and foolish.

Transport and Travel

air travel Air services in the USA are generally excellent and relatively inexpensive, and travel by air is a very convenient way of getting around such a large country.

There are often cut-price arrangements that are available for foreign visitors, especially if you book before you leave home, but these change from year to year, so you should check with a travel agent. There are also, from time to time, price-cutting wars and other competitive struggles between the different internal airlines, so make inquiries about what the best deals are at any given time. (American travel agents will normally be better informed about these than travel agents in Europe.) It may well be that some airlines are offering better prices or better arrangements than others for the particular journey you want to make.

Note that in America a return ticket is called a 'round-trip' ticket, and a single ticket is called 'one-way'.

the major internal airlines The major airlines for internal flights include American Airlines, Continental, Delta, Eastern, Northwest Orient, TWA, United, and Western. Airlines covering smaller areas of the country include Frontier (the West), Ozark (Midwest), Pacific (West Coast), Republic (the South and Midwest), Texas, and US Air (the Northeast).

American airports American airports are organized on a rather different basis from those in Europe. For obvious reasons (if you think about it) the international sections (if any) are very small, and the domestic sections (which normally include flights to Canada and Mexico) are very large by comparison. The larger airports, too, are organized by airline; each line has not only separate check-in desks but also separate gates, lounges or even terminals. It is especially important, therefore, to know which airline you are flying with.

Note that in the New York City area there are three main airports, Kennedy, La Guardia and Newark; in the Chicago area, O'Hare International and Midway; in the

San Francisco area, San Francisco, Oakland and San Jose; in the Los Angeles area, Los Angeles and Ontario; and in the area of Washington DC, Dulles International, Washington National, and Baltimore–Washington International.

At American airports it is very often possible for people who are not travelling themselves to accompany passengers on domestic flights right to the departure gate, provided that they also pass through the security check. Similarly, arriving flights can be met right at the gate.

Duty-free shops are often rather small (or even non-existent) and you usually have to pay for your purchases at the shop but collect them at the departure gate.

At very many American airports you have to *pay* for baggage trolleys by placing coins in a slot. This is a very foolish system to employ at the international airports where half the arriving passengers don't *have* any American coins.

getting to and from an airport

As in Europe, you can get to and from the larger American airports by bus and taxi. (At smaller airports buses may not always be available.) If you are driving to an airport, note that access roads can be very crowded, progress slow and parking difficult.

Taxis operate very much as they do in Britain, and at the larger airports there are 'dispatchers' who find you a cab and advise you about the fare. However, it is always a good idea to get an estimate from the driver of the cab of the fare before you get in. At some airports, taxi fares to common destinations are displayed on notice boards.

You will also encounter something called a 'limousine' ('limmo' for short). They may be vehicles standing outside the terminal that look like stretched cars, with three or four rows of seats, or minibuses. They will take you right to where you want to go, as a taxi would, but they will take all your fellow passengers right to where they want to go as well, and are cheaper. Alternatively, the limousine may be a normal but large and expensive car, taking up to five passengers, which will perform the same service but at greater expense. Very often it is also possible to arrange to be taken to an airport by limousine. You should telephone in advance (the day before your flight) to be on the safe side.

baggage   Baggage regulations are the same as for transatlantic
allowance   flights, and passengers are allowed to 'check' two pieces
                   of luggage each, regardless of weight, if they are of the
                   correct dimensions (see page 2). Misdirected baggage is
                   something of a problem on internal flights, so make sure
                   that your bags are labelled clearly.

checking in   When you check in at an airport you can, as in Europe,
                   request a smoking or a non-smoking seat. However,
                   current American law requires that everybody who wants
                   a non-smoking seat *must* be given one. In other words,
                   the non-smoking sections on aircrafts must be made
                   temporarily larger, if necessary, in order to accommodate
                   everyone who wants this type of seating. And even in
                   smoking sections it is not permitted to smoke cigars and
                   pipes.
                       It is very often possible to check in for a flight at the
                   departure gate if you are taking only hand baggage.

service on   Some internal flights are long — it takes seven or eight
board   hours to fly from Seattle to Miami, for example, and five
                   and a half hours to fly from Los Angeles to Boston.
                   Service on longer flights is very much like that on trans-
                   atlantic flights. Passengers are provided with meals, drinks
                   and films. The longer hauls usually offer first-class and
                   tourist ('coach') rates, though shorter flights are often
                   one-class only.

long-distance The two nationwide long-distance bus networks are
buses   operated by Greyhound and Trailways and provide a
                   very good way of getting around. The coverage of the
                   country is full, with good connections; the prices are
                   relatively low; and you get to see plenty of the country.
                   On the other hand, you should bear in mind that the
                   distances you want to travel may be enormous by Euro-
                   pean standards, and that it is possible to become bored,
                   tired and uncomfortable. The seats are comfortable,
                   however, and there is a reasonable amount of leg-room.
                   Buses are also air-conditioned and normally have toilets
                   on board (known, amazingly enough, as 'rest rooms' —
                   see page 81). Regular stops are made for changing or
                   resting drivers, picking up passengers and refreshment,
                   even during night-time journeys — in fact, you may have
                   to leave the bus from time to time so that it can be
                   cleaned. The buses have non-smoking sections, but in

such a confined space this is not much comfort to non-smokers.

Seasoned bus travellers recommend sitting half-way down the bus for the smoothest ride. Window seats may be cooler than aisle seats — sometimes too cool at night as the drivers turn up the air-conditioning to keep themselves awake.

You can, if you wish, purchase open-dated tickets from the bus station or a travel agent in advance, but for most trips it is neither necessary nor possible to make reservations. If there is not enough room for everybody, they simply put on another bus. If you have not bought your ticket in advance, you can buy one from a ticket desk at the bus station (not on the bus). *tickets and reservations*

Most often you have to check in and hand over your baggage, as you would at an airport.

Both the major bus lines issue cheap-rate passes giving unlimited travel for specified periods of time. These can be bought from travel agents in Britain or, at no extra cost, in America. They probably won't tell you this, but a Greyhound pass is valid on Trailways, and vice versa. *cheap-rate passes*

It has to be said that very often, especially in the big cities, American bus stations are very rough and unsavoury places, in which rather menacing and/or forlorn-looking people wander around — not necessarily the most pleasant of places for spending a couple of hours in the middle of the night. In some cities the bus companies have had to resort to the setting up of separate waiting areas for women and children. *bus stations*

The rail network in the USA is very inadequate and has become even less extensive in recent years in spite of the fuel crisis. Many routes simply have to be travelled by road or air. The routes that are covered, moreover, have very few trains on them (e.g. Chicago—Cleveland and San Francisco—Los Angeles — one train per day). By way of comparison, the journey from Los Angeles to San Francisco (about 400 miles: 645 kilometres) takes about one hour by plane, nine hours by bus and about ten hours by train (if it isn't late — see below). The well-travelled East Coast route from Boston to Washington, however, is fast enough, comfortable, and has **trains** a frequent service. (The Metro-liner trains on this route are especially comfortable, although you do have to pay a small surcharge on these trains.)

Most of the long-distance trains are run by Amtrak, a nationwide Government-sponsored body, which owns the trains and tries very hard. However, for reasons best known to the US Government, Amtrak does not own the tracks that the trains run on. These are owned, generally, by private companies. On some routes, therefore, the tracks are in poor condition, and the trains, as a consequence, are often late. Derailments, too, seem to be relatively frequent. Stations may be magnificent buildings in many cases but have a very run-down, empty and neglected feel to them.

Most Americans, especially away from the East, are not very used to travelling by train and are often not sure what they're supposed to do. (You can see them, for example, spilling tea in the dining-car because they don't realize that they should pick up the teapot *and* the cup when pouring.) There are often, therefore, lots of attendants, rather like air hostesses, to shepherd you around and answer silly questions.

tickets and reservations   Travelling by train in the USA is rather like travelling by air. For example, it is advisable on many routes, especially away from the East Coast, to buy your ticket in advance — most travel agents display Amtrak signs, and you can buy tickets from them. (This does not apply to commuter routes, which operate as in Europe.) Some long-distance trains are 'reservation required' trains; and you can make a reservation at the same time as buying your ticket (this can sometimes be done by phone). Having a reservation, however, does not mean that you are allotted a particular seat. It simply guarantees you a seat on the train — so, if you want to be sure of sitting with family or friends, get there early if you are boarding at a terminus. (You may even have to queue up to get on to the platform, or wait in a lounge, as at an airport.) On some long-distance routes, particularly in summer, it is a good idea to book well in advance. If trains are booked up no extra coaches are added — there aren't any. And, of course, if you want sleeping accommodation, you have to reserve that. Some trains offer 'roomettes', which are private sitting-bedrooms, plus a private toilet. If you come across the terms 'club car' and 'coach', note that the former refers to accommodation that is somewhat more luxurious than that available in the latter.

One thing you should know is that, again as at an airport, it is possible at larger stations and for longer journeys to check in any baggage you will not need with you on the journey. It then reappears at the other end. (If your luggage is large, it may be *compulsory* to check it in.)

your luggage

Once you get on, the trains are usually very comfortable, spacious and relaxing, though extremely slow by Japanese and British (but not Australian) standards — e.g. Edinburgh—London, four and a half hours, San Francisco—Los Angeles, ten hours, for roughly the same distance. Cleanliness is variable.

facilities on board

Smoking is often not allowed in the seating accommodation. (It *is* allowed, funnily enough, in the bathrooms, which can be quite spacious, at least on the older trains, with the toilet separate from the washing facilities and seats to sit on if you have to wait to get into the toilet. There are often separate bathrooms for men and women.) Smoking is also allowed, unfortunately for non-smokers, in the dining-car, in bars and in the domed observation cars, from which you can view the scenery on the more scenic routes — trips along the Pacific coast or through the Rockies can be really spectacular if your view isn't blocked by the smoke.

The dining-cars don't do a bad job, and you can often get drinks and snacks all day long in the bar-car. Note, though, that the alcohol regulations of the state you are passing through apply also on the train.

In spite of obvious inadequacies, then, Amtrak offers the possibility of covering large distances (e.g. Chicago to San Francisco, which takes two days) in comfort and without effort, and of seeing all the country in between rather than just a couple of airports at either end. However, train travel is not necessarily *cheaper* than air travel, especially if the airlines happen to be offering cheap rates on the route in question — and remember that you may need to have sleeping accommodation on the train. Amtrak, though, also has special offers which are worth taking advantage of.

These vary from New York (which even the tour guides tell you to avoid) through Boston which uses elderly rollingstock almost as high as an old-style tramcar, to

subways/ metro/ underground

Washington DC whose system is brand new and a delight
to use. Trains on all subways are non-smoking throughout.

Fares do vary, and you need to use the ticket
machines: but there are rarely any real people to check
your ticket. However, you do not need exact change
since there is often a 'bill-changer' which draws in your
dollar bill and produces $1 in change. Do not use older
bills — the machine will not accept them.

**trams and
trolleys**

Some cities (notably San Francisco and New Orleans)
still have streetcars — which are quieter than buses and
much more fun. The trip through the Garden District
of New Orleans is particularly good value at 80 cents.
Other cities (e.g. Boston, Austin and Salt Lake City)
have four-wheel buses privately owned and decked out
in colourful livery which look like 'trolleys' but are
mostly used for sightseeing trips.

hitch-hiking

This is probably not nearly such a good way of getting
around as it is in Europe. In some states, and in cities
or counties in other states, it is actually illegal. (The
American Constitution apparently does not guarantee
the individual freedom to ask for lifts by sticking out a
thumb.) And even when it is legal, it is usually harder to
get a lift than in Western Europe. Hitch-hiking is also,
apparently, quite dangerous — which may explain why
it is more difficult. The USA is a relatively violent
country (see page 82), and people are simply wary about
offering rides to strangers. Identifying yourself as a
foreign tourist (one couple carried a sign reading 'We are

Reproduced by courtesy of *Punch*

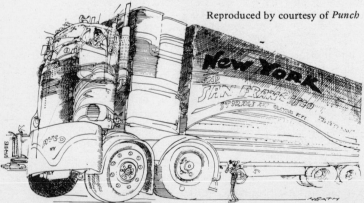

'*C'mon, good buddy, could you get me as far as New Jersey?*'

from Holland and not dangerous') may help you to get a lift, but it will not, of course, guarantee your safety. Rapes and murders of hitch-hikers are not as uncommon as one would like.

Hitch-hiking on motorways is, of course, illegal, but people seem to try it more often in America than in Europe — perhaps because they get desperate from waiting too long in legal places. You are allowed, however, to hitch-hike on motorway slip roads, at the point where they take off from the ordinary road, as in Europe.

Other problems are that American cities, with their urban motorways, underpasses, flyovers, ramps and intersections, can be a nightmare to hitch out of. And if you get left in a remote place, in some parts of the country you may be a very long way indeed from anywhere. Nevertheless, some people have had considerable success when hitch-hiking in the relatively less inhabited areas west of the Mississippi.

It is much better to arrange lifts in advance if you can and to share petrol expenses if necessary. Colleges, universities, YMCAs, YWCAs and other places frequented by young people often have boards on which people leave notes offering or asking for 'rides'. (See also 'drive-away' cars, page 27.)

cycling

While the rest of the world carried on cycling during the 1950s and 1960s, for the most part America forgot how, to the extent that even high-school children would drive to school. Recently there has been something of a renaissance in cycling, and in many areas it is a very useful way of getting around, especially where bike paths or bike routes have been established. You may well want to buy, hire or borrow a bike.

There are two important consequences of this earlier decline in cycling in the USA. One is that many people do not know how to cycle. That is, cyclists often behave more like pedestrians than motorists: they ride on the pavement or on the wrong side of the road; they ignore stop signs and traffic lights; they ride without lights at night; they give no hand signals. Also, car drivers often do not give cyclists a sufficiently wide berth. The other consequence is that cycling is regarded by many people not so much as a way of getting from A to B but as a way of life/form of exercise/symbol of ecological awareness/status symbol, etc. As a result, astonishingly large numbers of young Americans have ten-speed, drop-handlebar racing bikes. These are very light and fast and great if you are cycling long distances, riding up mountains or racing. At first, though, you may find them awkward for cycling in town, sight-seeing or shopping — they are expensive, uncomfortable and hard to control until you get used to them, and unsuitable for bumpy ground or stony roads. If you borrow one and have never ridden one before, you will find that you can get away with using just two or three gears, but you must remember to keep on pedalling while you change gear. Check which brake is which, too. The arrangement is sometimes the reverse of what it is on bikes in other countries.

There are also ordinary bikes around. If you get hold of one of these, you may find that the back brake works by pedalling backwards. This is perhaps safer than ordinary brakes when it is wet, but it seems generally to be less effective. This arrangement also means you can't pedal backwards while freewheeling or in order to get the pedals in the right place for getting on or moving off. Many Europeans are already used to this, but the British are not.

hand signals   One thing you should note is that the hand signals Americans are supposed to give differ from most other countries'. If you are turning left, you stick out your left hand, as we would do. But if you are turning right, you do *not* stick out your right hand. Instead you stick out your *left* arm and bend it at the elbow so your fore-arm is at right angles to the ground and your hand is about level with your head.

cycling on   For visitors from Britain, New Zealand, Japan etc., riding
the right   on the right is a bit awkward at first, especially when turning left and looking over your *left* shoulder to see if anything is coming, but you soon get used to it. Very often the safest way to turn left is to stay at the edge of the road, stop opposite the point that you want to cross to and then go straight over when the road is clear.

locking up   Do be very careful about locking your bike up. You will
your bike   notice many American cyclists carrying enormous chains for this purpose, and you will see that in many areas they take pains to pass the chain through the frame and *both* wheels *and* to attach the bicycle to something fixed

"Hell d'ya mean, 'Just taking a stroll'?"

Reproduced by courtesy of *Punch*

like a lamp post. You will even see people taking their
front wheel off and carrying it with them when they
leave the bike. Stealing bikes (especially ten-speed bikes)
is obviously big business.

Because of the sporting/exercise-oriented associations of   *cycling gear*
cycling, Americans very often wear sporting type clothing
when on a bike, and women very rarely wear skirts or
dresses. Many cyclists, very sensibly, also wear light crash
helmets.

There are some parts of the USA where walking is un-   **walking**
usual, difficult and the object of some suspicion. Pavements are non-existent or fizzle out; everybody drives
everywhere; and policemen may stop you and ask you
what you are doing if they see you walking. Areas where
this is particularly likely to happen include suburban
areas of places like Los Angeles, and the larger airports.

Hotels and Motels

Places called 'hotels' in the USA are likely to be of two main types. First, there are large, often expensive establishments, particularly in the big cities, which are typically frequented by the relatively wealthy, though it is also possible to find medium-priced 'hotel' accommodation. Secondly, there are small, often shabby, run-down establishments, which may be partly residential. These are typically inhabited by poorer people and have limited and shared facilities. Most tourists will therefore probably find themselves in motels or, in the cities, establishments calling themselves 'motor lodges' or 'motor inns'.

American motels make travelling around the USA, especially by car, very easy. There are many of them; they are easy to find; and you can more often than not find a room, even late at night.

As you drive along you will see many advertisements and signs directing you to motels, and these signs very often give prices as well. When you find a motel, you will usually see an illuminated sign outside which says 'Vacancy' or 'No Vacancy'.

choosing a motel

Members of foreign motoring organizations can obtain booklets from the American Automobile Association which list approved motels and their prices. They do not normally list the cheaper motels.

There are a number of area-wide and nationwide motel chains, and you may find you get to prefer a particular chain. Note, however, that prices may vary considerably from one member of a chain to another, depending on location, size, facilities and so on.

reservations

It is usually unnecessary to make motel reservations, especially if you are prepared to start looking for a room by about 5 p.m., as many Americans do, unless you are going to a resort area (e.g. southern Florida in the winter) or to a big event (e.g. Mardi Gras in New Orleans). But if you are going to the centre of a big city, it may be a good idea to stop on the outskirts and phone in. Note that it is possible, as long as rooms are available, to get a room in most motels at any time of the day or night.

If you are staying at a motel that is part of a chain, the receptionist will be happy to use the motel's telephone, telex or computer facilities to book you a room at other motels in the chain for subsequent nights.

A credit card is very useful for booking motel rooms by phone, which can often be done by calling toll-free numbers (see page 24).

prices

Prices are generally very reasonable by European standards, except in resort areas, and are normally basically *per room* rather than *per person*. Prices are generally quoted for single occupancy, with a small additional cost per additional person. This means that families and other groups willing to share a room can effect a very considerable saving by taking just one room. Most motel rooms have beds for four people (see below), and very often additional 'cots' — fold-up beds — can also be brought in. Five people in one room will cost not much more than one third of what they would cost spread over three rooms. Some motels take children and/or teenagers free when accompanied by their parents.

Breakfast is not included in the price of the room.

If you plan to stay in a hotel for several days, you may be quoted prices 'American plan' (including all meals) or 'European plan' (no meals included).

checking in

When you check in, the normal procedure in a motel (except in the larger, urban establishments) is to pay then and there. You will be given the key (some establishments ask for a 'key deposit', which they will return when you return the key), and then you drive to your room and leave your car immediately outside — in the case of motels with two or more storeys it is a matter of parking as near to your room as you can.

If you let someone carry your bags to your room for you at a hotel or motor lodge, they will expect a tip. In the USA people who perform this service are known as 'bell hops'.

your room

Motel rooms tend to be very similar wherever you go. There is little individuality or charm, but there are few unpleasant surprises either. Nearly all motels are clean and well appointed, although standards do vary, of course.

In most rooms, in addition to the bed or beds, there will
be a TV set (though often no radio) and a separate bathroom with toilet and shower (for tips on taps and showers,
see page 96). Soap, towels *and* face flannels are provided,
so there is no need to take your own. Facilities may also
be provided for heating water and making coffee in your
room, including sachets of instant coffee. There may also
be a fridge, and there will usually be an air-conditioner-
cum-heater. Most motel rooms also have telephones,
though this is not always the case. And there will probably be a Bible, whether you want one or not.

Very often motel rooms contain two double beds,
but some have one double bed and/or two single beds.
Double beds may be the normal size, 'queen-size' (bigger)
or 'king-size' (biggest). Single beds are known as 'twin'
beds, and there are even some rooms containing only
one 'twin' bed. Since the American terms for beds and
rooms can be a bit confusing for the foreign visitor, it is
as well, when you check in, to be specific about how
many of you there are and how many rooms and beds
you require. Some motels have suites, with more than
one bedroom sharing the same facilities, which are ideal
for families or small groups. Some rooms are advertised
as 'efficiencies'. These are rooms with a small kitchen, so
that you can cater for yourself.

When you arrive in your room, check in the drawers
to see what you can find. Menus, telephone instructions,
stationery, shoe-cleaning materials, plastic bags for wet
clothes and other goodies are often located there.

Don't be alarmed if you find a paper seal across the
toilet bowl in your bathroom, indicating that the toilet
has been 'sanitized for your protection'. This does not
mean there has been an outbreak of some dreadful disease
in the locality, merely that someone has been in to clean
your toilet. These seals are probably indicative of something important in the American psychology, but it is
difficult to know exactly what.

snacks and
meals
Motels do not normally have room service or restaurants
on the premises, although restaurants, bars and coffee
shops can be found at some of the larger hotels and
motor lodges. One of the joys of travelling in America is
going out for breakfast, and most motels are situated
close to restaurants that serve breakfast (see pages 59–
60), so that you can eat before you get on the road.

If you have meals in your motel restaurant (if there is one), it is normal practice to pay for each meal as you have it rather than ask for it to be charged to your room bill. In higher-class hotels, however, you can usually charge meals to your bill.

Many of the larger hotels and motor lodges are air-conditioned throughout, and have facilities such as shops, hairdressing salons and swimming pools on the premises.   **amenities**

Motels often provide washing machines and dryers for their guests, as well as vending machines for soft drinks and sweets — and ice. In your room there will be a small plastic bowl or bucket for use when collecting ice. The ice is normally, but not always, free. The idea behind these machines is that the majority of Americans are unable to drink even water without putting ice in it first (which must increase the country's energy-consumption enormously), and you too may be glad of it in hot weather. There may be an admonition on the ice machine that the ice is not to be used for filling coolers (see page 39). Many people use the ice from these machines for filling their coolers.

Some motels have provision for the playing of films, often fairly new releases, on your TV set. You do have to pay for this.

A few motels specialize in providing king-size water-beds and video porno films on the TV. You will want to watch out for these in order to avoid them or, as the case may be, not. (Sometimes you can also find *vibrating* beds.)

Eating . . .

Eating out is one of the joys of being in the USA. The food is usually good and often excellent; the prices are reasonable; and the service is mostly fine.

restaurants: first principles

choosing a restaurant

Some restaurants are open for breakfast; others are open twenty-four hours a day. A number of restaurants call themselves 'family restaurants'. Many of these serve no alcohol and have fairly restricted menus which include steaks, burgers, omelettes and sandwiches, all at very reasonable prices. They may also serve smaller and cheaper children's portions. Note that many American restaurants are 'specialty' restaurants. They may serve only, or mainly, steaks, seafood, etc.

when to eat

Many restaurants, especially the better-quality ones, open at about 11.30 a.m. (midday, rather than 1 p.m., is the most normal time for lunch in the USA), and some remain open until the evening, so it is possible to order a meal throughout the afternoon.

In many areas it is usual for people to leave work and go out for an evening meal at 5 p.m. or 6 p.m. rather than waiting until later. Consequently, outside the big cities restaurants tend to close earlier than they do in Europe.

reserving a table

Eating out is rather more popular in the USA than in northern Europe, and it is often necessary to make a reservation. You will sometimes see short queues of people waiting for tables at restaurants — it's more pleasant to wait in the bar, of course, if there is one — but these queues move quickly.

arriving at a restaurant

When you arrive at most restaurants other than 'truck stops' (transport cafés), you should *not* just go in and sit down — unless you see a sign saying 'Please seat yourself'. The normal thing is to wait for a 'hostess' or 'captain' to escort you to a table. Often there will be a sign that reads 'Please wait to be seated'.

Do not expect to share a table with other parties, even if the restaurant is crowded. It just isn't done.

Many restaurants have a no-smoking section, in some places by law.

One excellent American custom is that after you have sat down your waiter or waitress (or the 'bus boy' — he's the one who clears and sets the tables) will often automatically bring you a glass of water (with ice, naturally) and will keep on refilling it throughout the meal. (Most Americans are incapable of eating a meal without drinking something at the same time.)

When your waiter or waitress takes your order, it is not very normal for one person to order for the whole table. Each person orders separately, except in the most expensive restaurants.

You may find your waiter unusually or even obnoxiously friendly. He may ask you how you are (you're not supposed to tell him about your headache or bad back — just say 'Fine'), inquire whether you have had a good day and, later on, say that he hopes you will enjoy your meal.   *your waiter*

'Hi there! My name's Willard. I'll be your waiter tonight.'

'The Neighborhood', courtesy The Register and Tribune Syndicate, Inc.

To summon a waiter in a French restaurant you may call 'Garçon!' In Germany you may call 'Herr Ober!' In many American restaurants it is possible to summon your waiter by crying 'Bill!', or 'Mary!', or 'Claude!', or whatever. Waiters and waitresses often actually introduce themselves when they first come to your table (there is no need for you to reciprocate) or wear name tags, and you are permitted to use their first names (if you really want to) to attract their attention.

the bill

The bill (often called the 'check') comes usually with tax added but no service charge — though some restaurants do now add a service charge. The etiquette books say that you should leave a ten per cent tip for lunch, fifteen per cent for dinner. The tip should be calculated on the basis of the total *before* the addition of the tax.

At many restaurants you can ask the waiter to bring the bill and then pay at a cash desk on the way out.

how to eat: custom and practice

Americans eat funny. Alone in the world (even most Canadians don't do it), Americans eat everything they possibly can with a fork, and appear to work on the assumption that holding a knife in your right hand for longer than a few seconds is a gross breach of good table manners.

The system is that if it is absolutely necessary to use a knife, people take the fork in their left hand, if they are right-handed, and the knife in their right, and cut off a piece of meat or whatever it is in the normal manner (except that some people cut *behind* the fork rather than in front of it, which looks very odd). Then *they put the knife down*, transfer the fork to their right hand, and only then do they transport the food to their mouth. This is clearly ludicrous, but it is considered good manners.

There are several consequences of this system. First, if it is not absolutely necessary to use a knife, Americans don't use one, because obviously this greatly complicates things, and you will therefore see them trying to cut things like potatoes, fish and even bacon with a fork. Second, towards the end of a course, since only one implement is being used, food has to be chased around the plate with the fork — and for the last mouthful the thumb has to be used to keep the food in place, although one is not *supposed* to do this.

Third, tables are generally laid with one knife and two forks, the outside fork being for the salad. There is no need for foreign visitors to follow the American system and try to eat the salad with only a fork, but if you *do* use your knife, remember to save it for the meat course. Even desserts (except ice cream) are eaten with a fork if at all possible, and the spoon you see by your place is *meant* to be for coffee (but if you use if for your dessert no one will actually say anything).

This book does not recommend that visitors to the USA follow the American method of eating. One should obviously go along with the customs of a country that one is visiting as far as possible, but there are limits.

American restaurants (and homes) are very often without fish knives and forks. However, they do normally supply sharp steak knives when appropriate.

breakfast in America

If you're staying in a motel, you will probably go to a restaurant for breakfast. But even if you're not, breakfasting in a restaurant is a very enjoyable experience. (You may, of course, come across breakfast in American homes. You may stay with an American family, or be invited to people's homes, especially on Sundays, for 'brunch', which is a cross between breakfast and lunch. Brunch is also often available in hotels.) In any case, American breakfasts are different, in a number of respects, from breakfasts in other countries.

Americans have a strange tendency to mix sweet and savoury foods (see below the custom of eating jelly as a salad with meat), and this is very apparent at breakfast time. You may well be brought a single plate bearing bacon, eggs, pancakes, toast and jam. It is quite usual to combine pancakes and maple syrup with bacon and sausage, and the pancake syrup sometimes even finds its way on to the bacon.

You are also supposed to use the same knife for savouries and sweet things (except of course that Americans don't use knives unless they really have to), and you will even see people taking alternate mouthfuls of egg and toast with jam.

some breakfast dishes

If you order eggs in a restaurant, the waiter/waitress will ask you how you want them. You can reply that you want them 'scrambled' or 'boiled'. It is not sufficient, however, to ask for them 'fried'; you will have to specify whether you would prefer them 'sunny-side-up' (not turned over in the pan), '(turned) over' (fried on both sides), 'over-easy/easy-over' (turned over for a little while, with the yolk still a bit runny), or 'over-hard' (yolk set hard). If you order a boiled egg, it will probably not come in an egg cup. Boiled eggs are often served in a bowl, in which case you are supposed to cut the egg in half and spoon the contents into the bowl.

American sausage is often a Scottish-type sausage that comes in slices and is quite spicy. Link sausages are also available.

American bacon is not at all like British bacon. It comes in small strips, can be rather fat, and is served crispy. It is usually very tasty, and you can sort of eat it with your fingers.

'Hash browns' are shredded and fried potatoes. They are wonderful, especially with fried eggs and kitchup.

'Pancakes', sometimes called 'hot cakes', are not at all like English pancakes (which in the USA are called 'crêpes'). They are more like Scottish pancakes, made with baking powder, and are smaller and thicker than English pancakes. They are normally served in a pile, and you are supposed to put butter and syrup (maple or imitation) on them.

'Jelly' is jam and includes grape jelly, which is very tasty. Marmalade is not particularly common in the USA.

Toast is often served already buttered.

'English muffins' are a peculiarly American institution, though Americans assume, incorrectly, that British people know what they are. They are like small crumpets without the holes and are served toasted. You put jam on them. 'Muffin' is the American word for 'bun'.

A 'biscuit' is a smallish, scone-like bread roll, often served hot. You can get them at dinner time too. The British biscuit is, of course, known as a 'cookie' (sweet) or 'cracker' (savoury) — except that 'cookies' are often a good deal more cake-like than biscuits are.

Orange juice and coffee are frequently served with breakfast.

lunch and dinner

cocktails

It is much more usual to drink cocktails (see page 76) before lunch and dinner in America than in Europe and somewhat less usual, except in California, to drink wine with a meal. You can either have a cocktail in the bar, if there is one, while you wait for a table or for friends, or

you can have one served at your table before your dinner
comes. At some restaurants the waiter/waitress will
come to your table as soon as you sit down to ask if you
want a cocktail, and you can then drink this while decid-
ing what to order to eat. At others, there may be a separate cocktail waiter or waitress. In this case, you do not
normally order wine from him or her but from the
normal waiter — or the wine waiter (US: wine captain)
if there is one.

Do not hesitate to order Californian wines. They can
be excellent and in many parts of the country are cheaper
than European wines. Even some of the cheaper wines
are quite tolerable, particularly the drier white wines.

starters

Think twice before ordering an appetizer. At some
restaurants your meal may, in any case, automatically
include bread and/or salad, and portions are probably
generally larger than those you're used to.

salad

It is usual to have a salad with your meal, and a separate
plate is provided for this purpose. The normal practice
in America, except in French-influenced restaurants, is
to eat the salad *before* the main course — although it is

Reproduced by courtesy of *Punch*

not obligatory to finish it before the main course comes.
The waiter will normally ask you what sort of dressing
you want on the salad. The choice is usually: French
dressing (this is nothing like European French dressing
and is orange in colour), Italian dressing (oil and vinegar,
plus herbs), Thousand Island dressing (pinkish and
mayonnaise-flavoured), blue cheese dressing (often
called 'Bleu', as in French for 'blue'), oil and vinegar,
and sometimes a 'house dressing'.

A wonderful American invention is the *salad bar*, not
found in very many European restaurants. In restaurants
that have these salad bars the waiter does not bring your
salad. You go to the salad bar and help yourself, usually
to as much as you want. This is normally done after you
have ordered your meal; you eat the salad while the
main course is being cooked.

At the salad bar you will find chilled plates and many
salad items, some of which you may not recognize. The
stuff that looks a bit like cabbage, for instance, is probably
crunchy American lettuce, and 'bacon bits' are often
provided to sprinkle on the top of the salad. Americans
also have the bizarre habit of serving fruit jellies (jelly
is called 'jello' in the USA) as a salad or part of the salad,
and you might find these at the salad bar too.

choosing from   American menus can look rather confusing at first sight.
the menu   They are often laid out with an eye to impact rather
than ease of reading, and they tend to describe dishes at
length and in appallingly hyperbolic terms ('a succulent
portion of choice beef, broiled to perfection', etc.). They
also use terms which are unfamiliar to most English-
speaking visitors. Here are some points which may be
useful.

Fried mushrooms, fried onion rings and fried zucchini
(*zooKEEny*: courgettes) are sometimes served as starters.
They are fried in batter. You may also get, believe it or
not, fried potato skins.

Potatoes most often come 'french-fried' (= chips) or
baked. If you order a baked potato, the waiter will ask
you what you want on it. The choice is butter and/or
sour cream and sometimes chives.

Very often vegetables other than potatoes do not
come automatically with the meal, and you have to
pay extra for them, as indeed in many European restaurants.

'Scrod' (young cod or haddock), 'red snapper' and

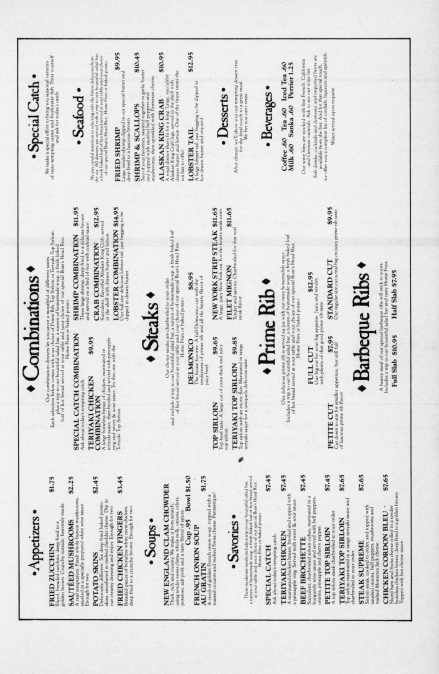

• Appetizers •

FRIED ZUCCHINI   **$1.75**
Sliced, breaded zucchini, deep fried to a golden brown. Crunchy outside, heavenly inside.

SAUTÉED MUSHROOMS   **$2.25**
A real temptation. Fresh whole button mushrooms, sautéed in a specially prepared white sauce. Enough for two.

POTATO SKINS   **$2.45**
Deliciously different. Six deep fried baked potato skins, smothered in melted cheddar cheese. Dip in our creamy dressing and enjoy. Enough for two.

FRIED CHICKEN FINGERS   **$3.45**
Breaded pieces of boneless white meat chicken, deep fried to a crunchy brown. Enough for two.

• Soups •

NEW ENGLAND CLAM CHOWDER
Cup .95   Bowl $1.50
This is the real thing. Made from scratch in our own kitchen, using tender sweet clams, whole milk, onions, celery, potatoes, salt pork and a tasty blend of spices.

FRENCH ONION SOUP AU GRATIN   **$1.75**
A crock of golden French onion soup, topped with a toasted crouton and melted Swiss cheese. Fantastique!

• Savories •

These moderate meals include a trip to our bountiful salad bar, a tureen of homemade soup, a fresh baked loaf of hot bread served at your table and our special Boar's Head Rice. Home Fries or baked potato.

SPECIAL CATCH   **$7.45**
Ask about today's tempting catch.

TERIYAKI CHICKEN   **$7.45**
A marinated chicken breast, broiled and topped with a pineapple ring. Served with sweet & sour sauce.

BEEF BROCHETTE   **$7.45**
Succulent, charbroiled sirloin cubes, marinated in a burgundy wine sauce and served with bell peppers, onions, pineapple and cherry pepper.

PETITE TOP SIRLOIN   **$7.45**
A top sirloin steak charbroiled to your order.

TERIYAKI TOP SIRLOIN   **$7.65**
Top sirloin marinated in a tangy teriyaki sauce and charbroiled to your order.

STEAK SUPREME   **$7.65**
Sirloin steak cooked to order and topped with sautéed onions, bell peppers, mushrooms and melted Monterey Jack cheese.

CHICKEN CORDON BLEU   **$7.65**
Sliced ham and Swiss cheese rolled in a tender boneless chicken breast, deep fried to a golden brown. Topped with hot cheese sauce.

• Combinations •

Our combination dinners let you savor a mouthful of different tastes. Each selection below comes with your choice of Prime Rib, Top Sirloin or Teriyaki Top Sirloin, plus a trip to our bountiful salad bar, a tureen of homemade soup, a fresh baked loaf of hot bread served at your table and your choice of our special Boar's Head Rice. Home Fries or baked potato.

SPECIAL CATCH COMBINATION   **$9.95**
Ask about today's tempting catch.

TERIYAKI CHICKEN COMBINATION   **$9.95**
A large boneless breast of chicken, marinated in teriyaki sauce, then broiled and served with pineapple ring and sweet & sour sauce. Try this one with the Teriyaki Top Sirloin.

SHRIMP COMBINATION   **$11.95**
Three large shrimp, deep fried to a delicate brown and served on a bed of rice with cocktail sauce.

CRAB COMBINATION   **$12.95**
Succulent flavorful Alaskan King Crab, served in the shell with drawn butter and lemon.

LOBSTER COMBINATION   **$14.95**
Our full size delicious lobster tail, just begging to be dipped in drawn butter.

• Steaks •

Our choice steaks are charbroiled to your order and include a trip to our bountiful salad bar, a tureen of homemade soup, a fresh baked loaf of hot bread served at your table and your choice of our special Boar's Head Rice. Home Fries or baked potato.

DELMONICO   **$8.95**
The house favorite. A full Delmonico cut with the tenderness of prime rib and all the hearty flavor of juicy beef.

TOP SIRLOIN   **$9.65**
Top beef taste. A large cut of extra thick and juicy top sirloin.

TERIYAKI TOP SIRLOIN   **$9.85**
Top sirloin with an exotic flair. Marinated in tangy teriyaki sauce for a uniquely delicious taste.

NEW YORK STRIP STEAK   **$11.65**
A large, juicy New York cut. For the hearty steak eater.

FILET MIGNON   **$11.65**
Tender and savory. Charbroiled for that real steak flavor.

• Prime Rib •

Our delicious prime rib is served au jus with our tasty horseradish sauce. Includes a trip to our bountiful salad bar, a tureen of homemade soup, a fresh baked loaf of hot bread served at your table and your choice of our special Boar's Head Rice. Home Fries or baked potato.

FULL CUT   **$12.95**
Our big cut for your big appetite. Juicy and tender, with plenty of that good prime rib taste.

PETITE CUT   **$7.95**
Cut down to size for smaller appetites, but still full of luscious prime rib flavor.

STANDARD CUT   **$9.95**
Our regular size cut is real big on juicy prime rib taste.

• Barbeque Ribs •

A hearty meal of our special barbeque ribs will stick to yours. Includes a trip to our bountiful salad bar and tasty Home Fries.

Full Slab $10.95   Half Slab $7.95

• Special Catch •

We make a special effort to bring you seasonal varieties of taste-tempting ocean and freshwater fish. Treat yourself and ask for today's catch.

• Seafood •

We pay careful attention to selecting only the finest delicacies from the sea. All dinners are served with a trip to our bountiful salad bar, a fresh baked loaf of hot bread served at your table and your choice of our special Boar's Head Rice. Home Fries or baked potato.

FRIED SHRIMP   **$9.95**
Large, tender shrimp dipped in our special batter and deep fried to a luscious brown.

SHRIMP & SCALLOPS   **$10.45**
Two of your favorites, sautéed together in garlic butter and topped with sautéed bell peppers and mushrooms, then sprinkled with Parmesan cheese.

ALASKAN KING CRAB   **$10.95**
A royal dinner that's fit for a king. Large, succulent Alaskan King Crab legs, served in the shell with drawn butter and lemon. One of the finest treats the sea has to offer.

LOBSTER TAIL   **$12.95**
A large lobster tail, just begging to be dipped in hot drawn butter and enjoyed.

• Desserts •

After dinner, we'll show you our tempting dessert tray for the final touch to a great meal. We bet you can't resist.

• Beverages •

Coffee .60   Tea .60   Iced Tea .60
Milk .60   Sanka .60   Perrier 1.25

Our wine lists are stocked with fine French, California and German varietals. Ask to see our wine list. Soft drinks, cocktails and imported beers are available from the bar. And for that special touch, we offer you a complete list of cordials, liqueurs and aperitifs. Water served upon request.

'mahi mahi' are all names of fish. 'Seafood' means
lobster, shellfish and fish, *including*, funnily enough,
freshwater fish! A 'seafood platter' may consist entirely
of fried fish and shellfish. If you do not like too much
fried food, ask about this before ordering. Note that
most Americans pronounce 'fillet' *fillAY* and 'filleted'
fillAYED, as if the words were French. Prawns are
known as 'shrimp' — (not 'shrimps').

These are some terms that may be unfamiliar:

gumbo	a type of soup made with okra, vegetables and meat or fish
grits	crushed maize
squash	various types of marrow
broiled	grilled
teriyaki	a tasty sweet and sour marinade applied to chicken or beef, plus a sauce with which the meat is served
au jus	this means that meat is served with a thin gravy made from its own juices. *Au jus* is French for 'with the juice', but many Americans do not know this and talk about 'the au jus'
crêpes	pancakes
à la mode	with ice cream.

American beef is usually good and often wonderful.
Try especially 'prime rib'.

American salt and pepper pots are confusing until
you realize that the salt pot may look like a pepper pot
except that the salt pot's holes are bigger. Pepper is
normally black rather than white. American mustard is
mild and normally eaten with hot dogs or hamburgers
rather than meat.

And that stuff in a dish that looks like ice cream is
actually whipped butter.

leftovers   You have probably heard that in American restaurants,
if you can't finish your meal (and you do get colossal
helpings), you can put the remains in a 'doggy bag' and
take them home. This is quite true. If you leave some
meat, in particular, your waiter may ask you if you'd
like him to put it into 'a little bag', or you can ask him
to to this. (These days the bag may actually be a
polystyrene (US: styrofoam) container.)

THE CHUTNEY KITCHEN

IN VINTAGE 1870 ● Yountville, Napa Valley

MENU

SALADS
Garden Salad 3.25
Tuna Salad 4.50
Shrimp Salad 4.95
Soup and Salad 3.45

SANDWICHES
Baked Ham 4.25
Smoked Tongue 4.25
Turkey 4.25
Cheese Board
  three cheeses, dry salami, & fruit . 4.65
Avocado & Cream Cheese 3.65
Turkey, Avocado & Cream Cheese 4.50
Salami 4.25
Tuna on Rye 4.25
Vegetarian 3.95
Cheese Sandwich 3.50
Soup in A Mug With Roll 1.50

*Choice of Cheddar, Jack, or
Swiss Cheese On Any Sandwich,
.40 Extra*

Vintage 1870 Food Services, inc.

DESSERTS
Chutney Pound Cake 1.25
Fresh Cheese Cake 1.65

BEVERAGES   Sanka 50
Coffee . . . . .50 Iced Tea 60
Tea . . . . .50 Homemade
Milk . . . . .75 Lemonade 75
Apple Juice . . . .80 Calistoga Water .95
Coca-Cola 65 7-Up 65

BEER AND WINE
Michelob . . . . 1.25 Steam 1.50
Coors . . . . 1.25 Heineken 1.50
  Red or White Wine by the glass . . 1.25
Small Bottle . . 2.25 Large Bottle . 4.25

CHILDREN'S SANDWICHES
(12 yrs & under)
Tuna 1.75
Cheese 1.75

Lunch Every day
Phone 707-944-2788

---

tea and coffee

Coffee in the USA is a relatively normal drink, while tea is, in some circles, somewhat more fashionable and of higher status — the reverse of British proletarian tea and posh coffee — though in the past several years there has been as big an upsurge in American tea drinking as there has been in British coffee drinking.

In some places you will be brought iced tea if you ask for tea, unless you specify that you would like it otherwise. You may also have to point out that you want milk in your tea (rather than cream or lemon) or even that you would like cold milk and not hot. Americans are actually hopeless at making tea, particularly in cafeterias and restaurants, since they do not understand that *boiling* water is essential in its manufacture.

In America it is not unusual for people to drink coffee *with* their meal, though it is also perfectly normal practice to have coffee afterwards. Many restaurants serve coffee in mugs rather than cups.

American coffee is normally excellent, and only rarely 'instant'. In most restaurants you can have as much as you like for the same price — they just keep filling your cup up at no extra charge. Coffee is served 'black' or 'with cream' (or 'with milk'). The term 'white coffee' is not used in most parts of the country. In most parts of America 'regular' (= ordinary, normal) coffee is black, and you may be served black coffee in some places unless you specify 'with cream'. (Boston is known, however, for the fact that its 'regular' coffee is white.) The term 'light' is also used to refer to white coffee. Many restaurants now serve caffeine-free brands of coffee, such as Sanka and Brim.

'ethnic' restaurants

The USA has a very wide range of 'ethnic' restaurants, many of which are rare in most parts of Europe. You may, for instance, encounter Vietnamese, Korean and Thai cooking. Indian restaurants, on the other hand, are much less common than in Britain and are rarely found outside the big cities.

Chinese food

Chinese restaurants in Britain, with some exceptions, mostly in London, are predominantly Cantonese — they provide food cooked in the style of Hong Kong and the neighbouring areas of the Chinese mainland. In the USA you are likely to encounter other types of Chinese food also, including especially Szechuanese and Mandarin cooking, both of which tend to be heavier and spicier than Cantonese.

Dishes are generally larger than those served in British Chinese restaurants. If you're not especially hungry, four people can make do with three dishes. You are also more likely to find chopsticks than in Britain.

A custom found in Chinese restaurants throughout the USA is that of bringing each customer a 'fortune cookie' together with the bill. The cookie is a small pastry containing a 'fortune' printed on a slip of paper.

Mexican food

A type of restaurant very popular in the USA but unknown to most Europeans is the Mexican restaurant. Mexican food is typically spicy, if often a little stodgy, and generally very inexpensive. Steak and chicken are served in many Mexican restaurants, but typically a Mexican meal will consist of some of the following:

tortillas	pancakes made with maize dough, which functions like bread or as a base for fillings (see below)
tacos	small, hard tortillas, often folded in half and filled with various ingredients
tostadas	crisp, fried tortillas covered with various ingredients
enchiladas	soft, rolled tortillas baked with a chilli sauce and meat or cheese filling
chiles rellenos	stuffed chilli peppers
frijoles	beans (*frijoles refritos* are 're-fried beans', which are mashed fried beans)
burritos	flour tortillas filled with refried beans or shredded beef, with a sauce and shredded cheese
sangria	a kind of red wine punch.

Beware jalapeno peppers (pronounced *halla-painyo*). They are *very* hot.

fast food

Fast-food chains, American-style, are currently on the increase in Europe, but many visitors to the USA will still be relatively unfamiliar with them. America itself abounds in fast-food 'restaurants', and the outskirts of many towns suffer from extensive ribbon development of neon-advertised establishments of this sort. The restaurants themselves are generally bright and clean.

Most of these places work on a similar principle. There is a long counter, above which is displayed a list (often with pictures) of the items available, and behind which several people (often students working for the minimum wage) are serving. Individual queues form in front of each assistant. You receive what you order more or less immediately and take it on a tray to a table, picking up things like straws, pepper, salt, ketchup, pickles and napkins (America is teeming with paper napkins) on the way. If you can't see any knives and forks, this means you are supposed to eat with your hands. If you can't see any straws, that's because they are hiding in the straw dispenser that you have to sort of fiddle with the bottom of to get a straw (one at a time) to emerge.

When you've finished, you yourself throw away *everything* (it's all paper and plastic) except the tray.

Many fast-food places have drive-in facilities. You place your order from your car via a microphone and then drive round to a special window to pay and pick it up. You may even encounter older-style places where a waitress brings your meal out, and you sit and eat it in the car from a tray hooked over the door through the open window.

You may be asked if your order is 'for here' or 'to go' (i.e. to take away). In some states there is no sales tax on food consumed off the premises.

names to look out for   The most widespread type of fast-food restaurant is that serving hamburgers. It includes the chains of McDonald, Burger King, Wendy, Burger Chef and Hardie's. Some of these restaurants also serve fried-fish 'sandwiches' in a 'bun' (a bread roll).

All the different chains have their own specialities, usually with self-explanatory names. A McDonald's 'Egg MacMuffin' for example, is an English muffin (see page 60) containing cheese, a fried egg and a slice of 'Canadian bacon' (a thin ham steak).

Arby's restaurants serve large roast beef, ham and cheese, and turkey 'sandwiches'. The meat in these is pressed rather than carved straight off a joint or bird.

There are a number of chains and restaurants, often with names containing the word 'Taco', which serve Americanized Mexican food (see page 66).

Some restaurant chains specialize in serving steaks quickly and cheaply, cafeteria-style — for example, Ponderosa, Bonanza.

And then there's Kentucky Fried Chicken. (Actually, to be fair, even if you don't like these places at home, you may find the American version more appealing.)

fish and chips   There are some genuine fish-and-chip shops run by expatriate Britishers or Australians, but these are few and far between. You are much more likely to come across 'fish-and-chip' chains, which are run just like other fast-food restaurants. You will not recognize the fish and chips as such, even though vinegar *is* available in these places (see below). The fish is fried in breadcrumbs or something similar rather than in batter and is frozen, pre-packed and mass-produced. The food, however, can

"And no French fries — ever."

Reproduced by courtesy of *Punch*

be quite OK, provided you pretend that it is something other than fish and chips.

Chips in America are called 'French fries' or 'fries' for short, and people ask for 'an order of fries'. (NB: in the USA 'chips' means crisps.) 'French fries' are normally thinner than chips, but 'steak fries' means 'fries' that are thicker, like British chips. Americans generally put ketchup on their chips, and you will not normally find vinegar.

'Fish-and-chip' chains also sometimes serve things called 'hush puppies'. You may come across these in other popular restaurants, too, particularly in the South. They are fried balls of cornmeal.

There are many speciality pizza restaurants in America, *pizzas* and many of them take telephone orders and deliver pizzas to your home, which can often be extremely convenient. American pizzas tend to be far superior to those available in Britain. They come in different sizes (often measured in diameter inches), and one large one can easily be big enough for a party of four people. If you want to share a pizza but can't agree on the ingredients, it is possible to order two different sets of toppings, one set on each half. Bars and some restaurants may also sell pizza by the slice. Most pizzas come with a thin crust ('American'), but some ('Sicilian', now known widely as 'deep pan') have thick crusts. The list of topping ingredients available varies but may be extensive and may include some things you might not expect, such as pepperoni (a type of small, sliced sausage) and anchovies.

ice-cream Shops selling large numbers of different flavours of ice-cream are beginning to appear in Europe, but are much more common in America. They are relatively easy to negotiate — you just pick what flavour(s) you want. But you may like to know that you can generally sample a small spoonful of a particular flavour to see if you like it. And you can either have your ice-cream in a 'cake cup'/'plain cone' (which is similar to what you get in Britain) or in a 'sugar cone' (which is crisper and sweeter).

You may encounter some flavours that you don't know or even understand. It helps, for example, to know that a pecan (many Americans say *pa-KAHN*; others don't) is a type of nut. It tastes rather like a walnut only better. (You find pecan pie in many places.)

'Sherbet' means a type of water ice with a low cream content (a sorbet).

soft drinks Fast-food restaurants do not serve alcohol. The soft drinks most often sold are Coca-Cola and Pepsi-Cola, plus fizzy drinks such as Seven-Up and Sprite (which are like lemonade) and root beer (which is like cough medicine). Fizzy drinks are known as 'carbonated beverages' or, more colloquially, 'soda', 'pop', 'soda pop', 'soft drinks' and, in some places, 'tonics'.

You may also be able to get iced tea, which is a very common drink in America.

All these drinks come with *lots of ice*. In fact, you will probably find as much ice as drink in your drink. The ice bangs into your teeth and makes them ache, gets in the way, and numbs your mouth so that you can't taste what you are drinking. If you ask for a soft drink without ice, they will think you're funny but will probably oblige. (They *may* charge you a bit extra, though — ice is cheaper than Coke.)

Drinks come in the following sizes: 'large' (enormous), 'medium' (large), 'small' (medium).

Milk shakes are made with ice cream as well as milk. They are therefore very thick, and you have a hard time drinking them. Sometimes a spoon would be more suitable than a straw. (NB: in the Boston area milk shakes are known as 'frappes'.)

delicatessen and bar food

There are many places other than chain restaurants where food can be obtained quickly and cheaply. Many bars, for instance, serve hamburgers — often tastier than those served by hamburger chains — and other dishes. And delicatessens ('delis') are excellent places for sandwiches and salads.

The sandwiches served in American restaurants, bars and delis are often enormous (and held together with cocktail sticks), and they are very adequate indeed as a meal. Sandwiches in these places, and in American homes, are often made with mayonnaise ('mayo') instead of, or as well as, butter and with crunchy American lettuce. When ordering a sandwich, particularly in a deli, you may well have to specify what sort of bread you want the contents 'on'. The choice is:

wheat	brown bread
rye	black rye bread
light rye	brown rye bread
white	white

A 'toasted' sandwich may well have bread that is lightly fried rather than actually toasted. 'Half a sandwich' means a sandwich made of two half-rounds of bread put together rather than two whole rounds.

Delicatessens are the hardest places to handle as far as terminology is concerned. Here are some explanations:

bagel	heavy bread rolls, often served with cream cheese
blintz	savoury pancake, often filled with cheese
BLT	bacon, lettuce and tomato sandwich
chicken/turkey/ tuna salad	*not* chicken/turkey/tuna and salad, but shredded chicken/turkey/tuna mixed with mayonnaise, etc.
chili	*chili con carne*, generally served in a bowl, with crackers, and eaten with a spoon

club sandwich	double-decker sandwich (with three slices of bread), often containing two types of meat — for example, chicken and ham
corned beef	*not* like British tinned corned beef, but slices of brisket treated so as to resemble salt beef
gyros	a Greek-style 'sandwich' of un-leavened *pita* bread and slices of pressed meat cooked on a spit and served with tomatoes, onions and sour cream
hero	large sandwich made with long French rolls (there are many different names for these in different parts of the USA — for example, 'submarine', 'grinder', 'hoagie')
lox	smoked salmon
pastrami	a type of spicy smoked beef
pickle	a pickled gherkin
pretzel	a thin, and usually twisted, salted bread stick (some are hard, some soft)
quiche	*quiche Lorraine* — egg and bacon flan
reuben	sandwich made with corned beef, melted Swiss cheese and sauerkraut, usually hot.

So that you don't feel too terrified and don't attract too much scorn from those who you are holding up in the queue behind, note that orders in a delicatessen tend to be given something like this: 'I'll have a pastrami on rye with mustard', or 'Give me a roast beef on wheat with lettuce and tomato, no mayonnaise, and a toasted bagel with cream cheese.'

cook-outs   Americans are very fond of barbecues, clam-bakes and other types of 'cook-out'. These can be good fun, and meat barbecued over charcoal can be delicious. However, you do sometimes have to be quite good at holding a plate in one hand, a fork in the other, and a glass in the other.

. . . and Drinking

In one respect American drinking laws are more liberal and sensible than those in Britain. Bars stay open all afternoon and are often open until 1 a.m., 2 a.m. or even later. However, in other respects American drinking laws are much less liberal and rational (and Americans in Britain complaining about pub hours should be firmly reminded of this).

It is difficult to give an accurate overview of American laws concerning alcohol because they vary from state to state, county to county and city to city. The following, though, may be noted.

Some towns, counties and even states are totally 'dry' — no alcohol is sold at all (apart from in private clubs), except that they allow the sale of very weak (3.2 per cent alcohol) beer, known as 'three-two' beer. Some places do not allow the sale of alcohol on Sundays, even in shops — you may find a bar locked over the alcohol shelves. You can see it but not buy it! Other places permit alcohol to be sold Sunday afternoons and evenings, but not Sunday mornings. (Note that this means sales have to stop at midnight on Saturday.)

In many parts of America, in spite of all those constitutional freedoms, you are not allowed to drink alcohol in a public place. That is, you may not sit in a park or walk along a street drinking beer, and you cannot even take a nice bottle of wine on your picnic. The severity with which this law is enforced varies considerably. In some places, people can be seen taking drinks in public places from cans wrapped in brown-paper bags. These are not cans of Coca-Cola. And in many states you are not allowed to drink alcohol while driving, or even have an opened alcohol container in the car.

Some bars have a licence only for beer and wine. Others are also allowed to sell spirits and thus, as Americans say, 'mixed drinks'.

Many bars have a period known as 'happy hour', often longer than an hour, when they sell drinks at lower-than-

alcohol and the law

when and where you can drink

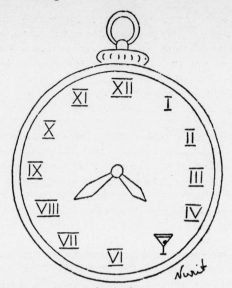

© 1980 Nurit Karlin, *Saturday Review*

usual prices. This is usually around 5 p.m. and may be only on certain days of the week.

In some bars it is possible to 'run a tab', which simply means that all the drinks at your table go on a bill, and you pay when it is time to leave.

the legal drinking age Legal drinking age varies from place to place but is generally between 18 and 21. Some places permit the consumption of beer at 18 but spirits only at 21. Others permit the consumption only of 'three-two' beer from 18 to 21. (Young people therefore often drive from one place to another with more liberal drinking laws, and then drive back less than sober. One cannot help feeling it would be better if drinking laws were uniform.) In any case, in some parts of the USA young people are allowed to vote, marry, raise families, hold down full-time jobs, be tried in courts as adults, join the army and even buy guns — but NOT (Heaven forbid!) have a glass of beer. In some places people aged between 18 and 21 are allowed to go into bars but not allowed to drink.

Another even weirder aspect of American drinking-age laws is that in some places people below legal drinking age are not even allowed to *sell* alcohol (after all, you can get very corrupted just by looking at a bottle of claret). This does not just mean that 'liquor stores' employ no 17-year-olds; it may also mean — and you must try very hard not to collapse in helpless giggles if you encounter this — that if you buy, say, a bottle of wine in a supermarket and the cashier is, say, a 17-year-old girl, she has to ask you or another cashier to press the ring-up button on the cash register for her for that particular item. (This is *absolutely true*.)

In most places these drinking laws are fairly rigidly enforced. You may, for example, find people queueing up to get into a bar and discover that the queue is caused by a 'guard' on the door who is asking *everybody* (including obvious old-age pensioners) for ID (identification — see page 10). If you ask him why he wants to know who you are, he will inform you that he actually wants confirmation of *how old* you are. *providing proof of your age*

On such occasions Americans often show their driving licences, which have their date of birth written on them. (The use of driving licences in this way has the bizarre consequence that some places issue non-driving licences to non-drivers so that they, too, can have some ID.) However, this presents a difficulty for British visitors, who, since Britain is — at least in this respect and for the time being — less of a police state than America, do not normally carry any ID. If you've got your passport on you, of course, you are OK, since this does give your date of birth. A British driving licence, on the other hand, doesn't — at least not overtly. You can try using it, however. The 'guards' are often so bemused that they will let you in anyway, and you can always explain that the expiry date is your seventieth birthday and let them do the arithmetic — if they believe you. In those places where it is necessary to distinguish between, say, 18- and 21-year-olds, you may also have your hand stamped as you go in to show how old you are.

American beer, with very few exceptions, varies from the mediocre to the terrible, and some brands even do a good job of upsetting your digestion. It is weak, fizzy and served chilled, which is just as well, since this takes the taste away. (This is not just prejudice against non-British beers. The Canadian beers available in America range from good to excellent.) **beer**

There are not many different *types* of beer in the US — 'light' and 'dark' are two terms commonly used. It is therefore normal to order beer simply by brand name: 'Two Michelobs', for example (cf. Americans in British pubs asking for 'a Watney's'). In a restaurant, in fact, it is quite all right just to order 'a beer', and they will tell you what they have. (Michelob, by the way, is pronounced *MICKLE-obe*.)

Lite beer is heavily advertised but not very nice, and is a low-calorie beverage designed for dieters.

It is not necessary, either, to specify quantity when ordering beer. If it comes in bottles or cans, you will get a bottle or can, and if it's 'on tap' you will get a glass, unless you order a 'pitcher' (i.e. a jug). The latter is a very convenient thing to do, since you can then take the jug and glasses to your table and keep filling up without going back to the bar. (It is harder, however, to keep track of how much you've drunk.)

Some beer comes in bottles with tops that look as if they need an opener, but you can, in fact, screw them off by hand — though you have to be careful not to hurt yourself on the serrated edges.

It is sometimes possible to find bottles of imported British beer, but this is expensive and, sadly, often kept on ice by the ignorant. It is also possible, in some stores and bars, to find a wide selection of beer from all over the world, especially Western Europe and Australia, and it is good fun to experiment with these.

Mexican beer is also good. You may be confused by the name 'Dos Equis', which actually means 'Two Xs' and therefore appears on bottle and menus as 'XX'.

cocktails   Cocktails and 'mixed drinks' are much more popular — and rather stronger! — in the USA than in Europe, and visitors may not be familiar with some of the terminology. 'On the rocks', as you probably know, means with ice, while 'straight up' or 'up' means neat and without ice.

There are hundreds of different cocktails, and there is no space here to list all the different names. The following, however, may be of some help:

Barcardi	to British people a type of white rum, but in American usage a cocktail of rum, lime and grenadine
B. and B.	brandy and Benedictine
Black Russian	vodka and coffee liqueur

Bloody Mary	a drink greatly superior to the one served in most British pubs, made with lemon juice, celery salt, tabasco and Worcester sauce, as well as tomato juice and vodka
Bronx	gin, vermouth and lemon or orange juice
John Collins	bourbon, lemon juice and soda
Tom Collins	gin, lemon juice and soda
Daiquiri	pronounced *DA-ckary*: a cocktail of white rum and lime juice, to which other fruit may be added (a 'frozen daiquiri' is a daiquiri that has been blended with crushed ice and is drunk through a straw)
Highball	any mixed drink made with a spirit plus water, soda water or ginger ale
Manhattan	a vermouth and whisky cocktail
Martini	not what you may think it is, but a mixture of gin and vermouth — and 'dry' martinis consist almost entirely of gin (if you want what British people call a martini, you will have to ask for a 'vermouth', pronounced *ver-MOOTH*)
Mint Julep	bourbon, mint and powdered sugar
Old-Fashioned	bourbon, bitters, sugar and a twist of lemon
Piña Colada	rum, coconut milk and pineapple
Rusty Nail	scotch and Drambuie
Screwdriver	vodka and orange juice
Whiskey Sour	bourbon, lemon and powdered sugar.

the hard stuff

In America 'whiskey' means bourbon unless otherwise indicated. Bourbon is a rather oily spirit made from maize. Rye whisky is called 'rye' and Scotch whisky 'Scotch'.

wine

In bars wine can often be bought by the glass or carafe. Don't be misled by names such as 'Chablis' or 'claret' — the wine is Californian. 'Chablis' is used to refer to white wine, and 'Burgundy' to red — Americans seem never to have heard of white Burgundy.

non-alcoholic drinks 'Punch' is a non-alcoholic drink made of fruit juices and lemonade unless otherwise specified. 'Spiked' punch contains alcohol.

Cider is also non-alcholic unless otherwise indicated.
For other soft drinks, see page 70.

In the City

Finding your way around American towns and cities is usually very simple, since most of them, as you probably know, are laid out as far as possible on a grid pattern, with streets for the most part going east—west or north—south. Moreover, if you have an address to locate, you can almost always tell where it is because, starting from some central point in the town, each 'block' is the 'hundreds block', the 'two hundreds block' and so on. Thus 705 Colorado Street will be seven blocks north, south, east or west of this central point. If the address is 705 N. Colorado Street, you will also know that it is north of the centre. (You will even be able to work out how far away the building is, because blocks are generally of the same size.) All the other buildings 'on' the same block will also have numbers in the 700s, and all streets running parallel to Colorado Street will have their 700 blocks at the same level.

finding your way about

If there are only five buildings on one side of Colorado Street, on that particular block, they *may* be numbered, say, 705, 711, 727, 733 and 779, and there is certainly no guarantee that a number 711 will be flanked by 709 and 713. (On the other hand, 711½ will be between 711 and 713.)

If a street is interrupted at some stage by, say, an extra large building or park, the name of the street after the interruption is likely to be the same as that before the interruption.

Americans very often omit the words 'Street', 'Avenue', 'Drive' when they give directions or supply addresses. You will hear people say 'on Colorado at 1st' (i.e. on the corner of Colorado Street and 1st Street), or 'on Colorado between 1st and 2nd', or 'I live at 705 Colorado'.

interpreting directions

Distances and directions are often given in 'blocks' — for example, 'two blocks north and then one west'. (Compass points are referred to in directions much more frequently than is the case in Europe — it is easier, of

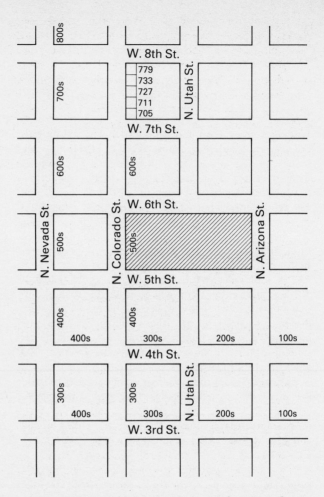

course, to know which way north, south, east and west are in American towns.)

apartment and office numbers

Note that the symbol # means 'number'. It is often used in addresses like this: '1212 N. Colorado, # 205', which is the same as '1212 N. Colorado, Apt. 205' and refers to apartment number 205 in the building at 1212 Colorado Street.

Apartment, room and office numbers are normally arranged so that the 100s are on the ground floor (which in the USA is called the 'first floor'), the 200s on the first floor (the 'second floor'), and so on.

Buses and trains operate very much as they do in Europe, **getting about**
except that bus services in most towns tend to be much **the city**
less comprehensive; see also pp. 47—8.

Most bus services operate on the basis of a single,
fixed-rate fare. Usually you pay the driver as you enter
the bus. You often have to tender the exact fare. Generally you get on at the front of the bus and leave from a
door situated in the middle or at the back, but it is also
very often possible to leave from the front too. Some
exit doors open only when you step down on to the inner
step. Transfers from one bus to another are often possible;
a small charge may be levied, though often transfers are
free.

In some areas laws against jay-walking are fairly strictly
enforced. In these areas it is not a good idea to cross the
street against a sign that says 'DON'T WALK' or anywhere in a town centre other than at a street corner.
Watch to see what the locals do.

There is an unwritten rule in many parts of the USA
that requires you to *walk on the right* when the pavement is busy. (This also seems to apply to stairways.)
The practice is obviously a very good one and cuts down
on bruises and frustration.

If you are spending any time at all in a town (or any- **toilets**
where else for that matter) you will need to find a toilet.
These are quite hard to find — for two reasons.

The first is that there are few public toilets in the
USA (although restaurants and stores, naturally enough,
do have them). Where you do find them you will not
usually have to pay — this is a barbaric European custom
— though there may be a few pay cubicles (which are
normally cleaner) as well as free ones. The second reason
is that they will not be labelled 'toilet'. For some reason,
many Americans find the word 'toilet' offensive, and you
will therefore have to watch out for euphemisms. These
include 'bathroom' (but don't expect a bath), 'rest room'
(but don't try to rest there), and (we hesitate to print
this) 'comfort station'. If you can't bring yourself actually
to say these words, you can ask for the 'men's room' or
the 'women's/ladies' room'.

Americans do not go in for building substantial
cubicles in public toilets, so if you prefer peace, quiet
and total privacy, you're likely to be disappointed.
Indeed, particularly in men's toilets and especially in

bars and at roadside toilets, the cubicles are fairly likely not even to have doors. This peculiar custom seem to be due to (a) vandals, (b) poverty and (c) excessive fear of what people might get up to behind locked doors. So be warned.

You can't always expect to find cleanliness, towels, toilet paper or other similar luxuries either, but this depends on the respectability of the establishment. On the other hand, you may in some places find that paper seat-covers are available ('for your protection'). Women are warned not to put their handbags on the floor, since thieves can reach in and steal them.

violence and safety

Some American cities have extremely high crime rates, as you probably know, and American crime levels generally are astonishing by European (let alone Japanese) standards. You will constantly encounter evidence of this in many urban areas — the bars over shop windows, the numerous enormous locks on doors, and so on.

It is something you have to think about. The vast majority of Americans, of course, manage to get through each year without being mugged or raped, but there really are some areas of some cities where it is not wise (particularly for women, unfortunately) to walk alone at night or even, occasionally, in daylight. Many American cities, too, are segregated residentially, particularly in the inner-city areas, so that Anglo-Saxons, blacks, Hispanics, Italians and so on all live in their separate neighbourhoods. The dividing line between these neighbourhoods can be very sharp, and in some cities you should be careful. It is not wise in some places for white people to venture into certain black areas, and vice versa. In other cities there are no problems — ask the locals.

The most frightening people you will probably see, however, are the police. Most American policemen are probably very nice, but they don't look very friendly. They all carry guns — as, indeed, do even security guards in shopping centres — and in some states, believe it or not, it is legal for police to shoot at suspected criminals *just because they are running away*. Be careful. Don't run away.

In fact, *many* people in the USA have guns; to an extent that seems lunatic to even the most bloodthirsty European. And the consequences of this are considerable. In 1979, 10,000 people were murdered by hand-guns in

© Steve Kelley; © 1985 San Diego Union Copley News Service

the USA (not including people shot by the police). There were also about 10,000 other murders. You are thus more than ten times more likely to be murdered in America than in Britain, though most victims are murdered by people who are related or known to them, so tourists don't have to worry too much. But tourists *do* have to worry about mugging and theft in certain areas. Again, ask the locals for advice. If you do as the locals do, you should be OK.

Some towns have a *curfew*. This is not as alarming as it sounds, even though it is a little odd. It is simply a law stating that children under a certain age must not be on the streets unaccompanied after a certain hour.

Mail

The American Post Office is a much maligned institution, and it does not, in fact, seem to work terribly well in some respects. It is also one of the few nationalized concerns in the USA, which may be why many Americans are petrified of 'socialism'.

Note that post offices are just post offices. There is no tendency, as in Britain, for the smaller post offices to double as newsagents, tobacconists and confectioners.

addressing envelopes

Americans normally put a return address on the outside of envelopes, in the top left-hand corner, when posting letters. If you hand over letters for posting at a post office, you may be told to do the same.

All American addresses include five-figure 'zip codes', which operate rather like British and Canadian postal codes but refer not to individual postman's walks but to towns or sections of large cities. Mail posted without a zip code will still arrive, but the zip code is said to speed things up. The codes go numerically, very roughly, from east to west, with numbers in the Northeast beginning with 0 and those in California beginning with 9. In many areas, four extra digits are currently being added to zip codes to give postmen more detailed information as to where an address is, and make it harder for everyone else to remember.

buying stamps

Stamps can, naturally enough, be bought at post offices, but they can also be bought elsewhere, particularly from vending machines in places like hotels and supermarkets, though you usually have to pay a little extra in this case, which is annoying.

posting a letter

Obviously enough, you can post things at post offices and in street-side post boxes. Post boxes can be hard to spot if you don't know what you're looking for. They tend to be on street corners; they are blue, and they look like litter bins. If you see a blue litter bin, it is probably actually a mail box. If you are over 5 feet

11 inches (1.80 metres) tall, you will not be able to see how to get your letters into the mail box, unless you bend down and look. There is, in fact, a flap with a handle that you pull back to reveal a space into which you drop your post, but this handle is obscured from view by the top of the box. There are also drive-up mail boxes outside post offices and elsewhere, so that you can post letters without leaving your car.

If you are staying in an American house, you may find that it is possible to post letters without going out: the postman will pick up letters left in your mail box for mailing at the same time as he delivers your post. Many houses have mail boxes by the roadside, so that the postman does not have to come up the drive. There is often, in such cases, a 'flag' (a metal arm) on the box, which can be raised to show that you have post to be picked up, so the postman will check your box even if he has nothing to deliver. Apartment blocks, too, frequently have rows of mail boxes in their entrance halls, so that the postman does not have to deliver mail individually to each flat, and mail for posting will often be picked up from these areas.

posting a parcel

Trying to post parcels at an American post office is rather like taking an exam, and there are many things they can fail you on. In some areas they will *not* accept parcels done up with string; they will *not* accept parcels unless they are boxed; they will *not* accept parcels done up with Sellotape (scotch tape); they will *not* accept parcels done up with masking tape; they will *not* accept parcels wrapped in anything other than dark brown paper; they will *not* accept very small parcels; and they will *not* accept Kodak's little film envelopes. In fact, you get the distinct impression they don't really want you to post anything at all. If you want to have your parcel accepted, you must do it up with brown tape or 'strapping tape' — which can be bought at stationers. In other areas the Post Office's regulations are interpreted more liberally. If in doubt, phone the local post office and ask.

registered mail

Registered mail is available in America, as in Europe. It is also possible when sending mail to ask for a 'certificate of delivery', which is something like recorded delivery, but you actually receive through the mail confirmation that your letter or packet has been delivered.

telegrams   You cannot send telegrams from a post office. Telegrams are handled by Western Union or other private firms. They can generally be sent by phone — look in the Yellow Pages.

receiving mail   In most places there is only one mail delivery per weekday, and this may come as late as mid-afternoon.

If people are writing to you in America at someone else's address, it is a very good idea indeed for them to put 'c/o' on the envelope, since American postmen have been known to take things into their own hands and return mail to the sender because they *know* that you don't live at that address.

Shopping

In many areas of the USA you have to travel a lot further to go shopping than in Europe. There are fewer neighbourhood shops, and even town-centre-type stores have in recent years been moving out to suburban shopping centres or 'malls' (pronounced *mawls*), so a car becomes essential. In the winter, however, these malls are a delight in the colder parts of the country, because they are mostly enclosed, and in the summer the air-conditioning is very pleasant. They also normally provide drinking fountains (as do office blocks and other public buildings) supplying clean, cool water -- an excellent idea. Notice that in malls, as elsewhere, Americans do not normally walk up or down escalators. They just stand patiently and wait to arrive.

Shopping is generally a lot easier and more relaxing than it is in Europe. Shops are more spacious and less crowded, and shopping hours are longer. Many shops are open in the evenings and on Sundays, and some grocery stores are open twenty-four hours a day, seven days a week.

Shop assistants (US: clerks, pronounced to rhyme with 'perks') are generally very friendly and helpful. Sometimes they are too helpful — you can get pounced on as soon as you walk through the door. And sometimes they are too friendly — they may inquire after your health (cf. waiters) and hope you have a nice day when you leave. But, generally speaking, they look after you well and, unlike, say, their British counterparts, treat you as if you were a human being.

One initial difficulty with shopping in America is sales tax. Since the rate of sales tax varies from place to place, and since the goods that are to be taxed also vary (in some places, for example, food is not taxed, while in others it is), prices shown and advertised are always *before* the addition of tax. In other words, you often have to pay more than you think, and it is no good

sales tax

getting out $5.00 to pay for something that costs $4.95, because the actual cost will be something like $5.25.

goods at a discount If you hear that something is 'on sale', this does not just mean that it is being sold. It means that it is in a sale, being sold at a reduced price.

A 'white sale' is a sale of sheets, towels and tablecloths, etc.

tokens There is, unfortunately, no national system of book tokens or record tokens in the USA, so you just can't buy such things. Some individual stores do issue gift certificates, however.

drug stores Drug stores are amazing institutions, where you can indeed buy 'drugs' and have prescriptions made up, but they generally also sell a wide range of other goods, including magazines, hardware, stationery, etc. They are rather like glorified versions of Britain's Boots stores, but they sometimes have a counter at which food and drink are sold as well.

buying clothes It is quite easy to get into a muddle buying clothes in the USA. One difficulty is that some of the terms that are used are different from those found in British English. Here are some examples:

panty hose	tights
hose	nylons
tights	thicker black or coloured tights (like those dancers wear)
pants	trousers (the word 'trousers' is also used and understood)
underwear	underwear (but often used to mean simply underpants/panties)
vest	waistcoat, sleeveless pullover (as worn by men and women); a vest is called an 'undershirt'
jumper	type of dress worn over a blouse
(bath) robe	dressing gown (also known as a 'house-coat' in the USA)
nightgown	nightdress
overalls	dungarees.

For comparative clothing sizes, see page 137 – but note that American clothes are cut rather larger than British clothes, so if you are 'large' in Britain, you may be 'medium' in the USA.

Some American men's shirts come in different sleeve as well as collar sizes, which can be highly convenient.

There are relatively few local grocery shops in America and hardly any greengrocers or butchers in suburban areas in many parts of the country. You have to go to the supermarket for most food items. And it is in the larger supermarkets that it is possible to see how affluent the USA is. The range, size and quality of goods is impressive.

© M. Stevens

For the most part, supermarkets are operated as elsewhere. Things to bear in mind are:

1   Fruits and vegetables are usually displayed and sold on a help-yourself basis. You snap plastic bags off a roll and put the fruit you select into them.

2   You don't have to take your own shopping bag to the supermarket (though, of course, you can if you like) because you will be provided with large, strong, brown-paper bags at the checkout.

3   You don't have to pack your own bag at the checkout. They will do it for you. In many supermarkets you can actually have your purchases taken to your car for you.

4   Most people pay by cheque. If you want to pay by cheque, therefore, you don't have to worry about holding up queues of impatient cash payers behind you. In some stores you have to go to a special desk to have your cheque approved before going to the

checkout queue. Some places will take your cheque only if they have previously issued you with an ID card. (For cheques, see also page 9.)

As can be imagined, these features mean that doing your grocery shopping in the USA is a good deal more relaxing than it is in Europe. One wishes supermarket managers in Britain could see fit to introduce some of these helpful facilities for *their* customers.

meat Lamb is less common in America than in Europe, but meat generally is excellent, especially beef, which ranges from good to wonderful. Many of the names used for cuts of meat are different from those used in Britain and Australia. American bacon (see also page 60) is sold in large packets containing thin, fatty slices. It doesn't look very appetizing, but if you can find some that isn't too fat, it is actually very nice.

fruit and Fruit and vegetables are known collectively in the USA
vegetables as 'produce' (pronounced *PROE-dooce* or *PROE-duce* by most Americans). American lettuces come in many shapes and sizes, but you are most likely to encounter hard, crispy 'iceberg' lettuce. Softer lettuces of the type more common in Britain are 'leaf', 'bib' or 'Bibb', and 'Boston' lettuce. Note that Americans say not 'a lettuce' or 'two lettuces', but 'a head of lettuce' and 'two heads of lettuce' — in American English you can't say 'one lettuce' any more than you can say 'one bread'. Spring onions are widely known as 'scallions'. Tomatoes are very often much larger than British people are used to, but there are also much smaller tomatoes, known as 'cherry tomatoes'. Sweet potatoes are widely available. For 'squash', see page 64.

milk Most American milk has vitamin D added to it. It is most often sold by the quart or half-gallon. Skimmed milk is readily available, as is yoghurt and sour cream. Double cream is known as 'heavy whipping cream'.

bread A confusing number of different varieties of bread are available. Bread is nearly always wrapped and very frequently sliced. Much of it is refined to death, but good wholemeal bread is also sold everywhere although there is a strong tendency for it to be far too sweet.

'Baked goods' is a general label used for bread, buns, pies and cakes. If you want pastry, look for *dough*. (*Pastry* means cakes and buns.)

American mustard is more like French or German than English mustard. It tends to be sweet and very mild.   *mustard*

Much of the wine sold (see also page 77) is from California or New York, though you will also find many European and Australian wines. Californian wines can be excellent, and most of those sold in supermarkets are quite tolerable. As you might suppose, the wine sold in screw-top bottles is less good than that sold in corked bottles.   *wine*

   American producers do not adhere to the labelling conventions in force in Europe. Thus 'sherry' may well be made in California, and Californian 'Burgundy' has, obviously, never been anywhere near France — it is simply a label used to indicate what the manufacturers believe to be a Burgundy-type wine. American 'port' is nothing like you are used to either.

There are, naturally, a number of things you can never or only rarely find in the USA. For the British, these include English mustard, marmalade, orange squash, Marmite and pickles. (When Americans talk about pickles, they mean pickled gherkins, not real pickles.) You'll probably manage without them for a while.   *what you probably won't find on the shelves*

At Home with Americans

Americans are very hospitable (see page 139). Even if you are a tourist, you may end up being invited to somebody's home. And, of course, if you are staying in the USA for any length of time or exchanging a house with an American family, you yourself may actually be in charge of an American home. Americans, incidentally, live either in a house, which tends to be called a 'home' (e.g. 'She has a very nice home'), or in an apartment (i.e. a flat), or in a 'condo', which is short for 'condominium' and means, basically, that the inhabitant buys rather than rents the apartment — though it's a bit more complicated than that.

It is foolish to generalize, but the decor in American homes tends to differ from that found in British homes, for example. Fittings are often plusher and more ornate — plastic flowers in the bathroom are not entirely unknown.

Especially in surburban areas, Americans like to go in for do-it-yourself, private-enterprise jumble sales. They do this if they are moving house, if they have a lot of junk to get rid of or simply because they want to make some money. These sales are often known as 'garage sales', although they are not necessarily held in the garage. Other similar affairs are 'apartment sales' and 'yard sales'. They are all very good occasions for picking up bargains, especially if you have just arrived and want to get stocked up with odds and ends. They are advertised in the local press and around the neighbourhood.

electricity

current

Electrical current in the USA is only 110 volts, so it is more difficult to electrocute yourself, but it also means that there is no point in taking European appliances with you — not even your hair drier — unless they are equipped for dual-voltage use.

Electricity meters are very often located *outside* the house or apartment, so you don't get disturbed every time they want to read your meter (and they do read it — and send you your bill — every month).

Drawing by Sempé © C. Charillon, Paris

Strangely enough, many living-rooms and bedrooms do *lights and*
not have ceiling lights (US: overheads), although these *switches*
are normally present in other rooms. In living-rooms
wall switches often operate wall sockets that are some
distance away from them and below them. Wall switches
normally go *up* for *on* and *down* for *off*, which can be
confusing at first.

Standard lamps, bedside lights and other lamps often
have two- or three-way bulbs, which give two or three
degrees of brightness. (Bulbs are much easier to instal
than in Britain — you just screw them in.) Very often
lamp switches have to be turned in a clockwise direction
rather than pushed, and they lock into position (bright,
medium, dim or off).

Many Americans have electric over-blankets on their beds. These are thermostatically controlled, and are supposed to be safe to leave on all night.

appliances and plugs
Appliances all come, sensibly enough, with plugs already fitted, so you don't have to fool around with wiring up plugs. Most plugs have two blades rather than pins.

record playing
If you have access to record playing equipment while you are in the USA, you may observe that American 45 r.p.m. records do not have middles — you can either buy snap-in centres or use a small disc that you place over the spindle.

locks
Many of the locks on external doors that look like Yale-type locks aren't. You need a key to lock them as well as to unlock them. Outside doors (see 'violence and safety', page 82) very often also have chains on the inside that permit you to open a door to see who's outside without totally unlocking it. Inside doors frequently have locks that are operated by pressing and/or twisting a button in the centre of the door knob or by pushing and twisting the knob itself.

curtains
In very many middle-class American homes, curtains (also called 'drapes') are operated by drawstrings located at the side of the window. Europeans are not unfamiliar with this system, but it is a lot more prevalent in America. The system is supposed to make drawing the curtains easier, but it often has the disadvantage of being less flexible. It may be, for example, that you cannot close just one of the curtains if you want to (to keep the sun out, for instance) without closing the other.

central heating
Most American homes have central heating, typically oil- or gas-fired hot air or radiator systems, or electrical underfloor or overhead systems. Very often there is only one thermostat for the whole dwelling, and in many places you will find a combined heating and cooling system, operated from a single thermostat.

During the worst part of the winter in the colder areas, the air can often be very dry, and central heating systems can make the air even drier. One way of combating this is to employ a humidifier. These are of different degrees of sophistication, but basically you fill them with water and they emit a very fine spray of moisture into the room.

In the parts of the USA where it gets cold in the winter, most houses have forms of double-glazing. Often there are simply two sets of windows, the outer set being known as 'storm windows' (which can be left open or removed during the summer).

double-glazing, storm windows and screens

In most areas of the USA mosquitoes, flies and other insects can be a serious problem in the summer (see page 19), so most houses have fine-mesh screens over the windows and outside doors. In the colder areas, therefore, you may find three layers of 'window' to cope with (inner window, screen and storm window), though in many cases you cannot have the screen and the storm window in at the same time.

In most areas of the USA it gets so hot and/or humid in the summer that very many homes have air-conditioning (known by some Americans as 'AC'). There may be a central unit that cools the whole place from one control. If not, there will be individual air-conditioners in some of the rooms, fitted into the window or wall. These consist, basically, of a fan, which blows air into the room, and a cooling system, which the air passes through on its way into the room. The fan can often be adjusted to operate at different speeds and can also be switched on separately from the cooling system.

air-conditioning

The cooling system can be adjusted for temperature. There may also be a vent which can be opened when the air-conditioning is not in use to let air into the room.

One common-sense point that people unused to air-conditioners do not always think of is that when you switch the air-conditioner on, you should also shut the windows and doors to keep the hot, humid air out.

Air-conditioners can be noisy, and if they have them on at night some people have to resort at first to earplugs in order to get to sleep. Eventually, though, you get used to it.

Some households have de-humidifiers for use in damp or muggy weather. These extract moisture from the air, and you have to empty the water out of them from time to time.

bathrooms 'Bathroom' in the USA often means 'toilet', but as most houses have the toilet and bath/shower in the same room, no confusion arises. What is confusing is the term 'half-bathroom' or 'half-bath', which Americans, comically enough, will tell you means 'a bathroom without a bath' — it has a toilet and basin and sometimes contains a shower.

Like American motels and hotels, American hosts provide visitors not only with towels — just help yourself from the pile — but also with face flannels, so there is no real need to pack your own. Americans haven't got the faintest idea what 'flannel' or 'face cloth' mean and instead use the word 'washcloth'.

People sometimes do not fit locks to their bathroom doors, for reasons best known to themselves. The convention often is that the door is left open unless the bathroom is occupied.

taps American taps (US: faucets) can be a little confusing, since some arrangements, though found in Europe, are less common there than they are in the USA. One frequent American arrangement is to have the flow of water regulated by a handle that works on a universal joint arrangement, such that an up-and-down movement determines the flow and a left-to-right movement determines the temperature. American taps are very consistent — right is cold and left is hot — but if there are separate taps in the shower, make sure you know which way they turn. Sometimes both taps turn in the same direction; sometimes they turn in opposite directions. If you get it wrong, you can scald yourself. There will also be a device to convert the flow from 'bath' to 'shower' — it is often a knob that has to be lifted. If you do not think you are going to pass this particular intelligence test, get someone to show you what to do before you take your clothes off.

Very often there is only a single spout through which mixed hot and cold water runs into the bathtub or basin. This has the advantage that you can wash your hands in running water of the desired temperature, but it has the disadvantage that if you want cold water after you have been running hot, you have to wait a few seconds for the hot water still in the pipes to run out and for the spout to cool down. Note, too, that some taps have to be pulled and pushed rather than turned, and that there may be a lever (pronounced *levver*) instead of a plug.

Most American homes have at least one shower, which is nice, but the shower is often combined with a bath, which isn't. The bathtub may well be small, uncomfortable and not deep enough for a proper soak (hence, perhaps, the popularity of hot tubs — see below). If you're not too practised at taking showers, remember to place the shower-curtain *inside* the tub so that water does not splash all over the floor. And remember too, after your shower, to leave the curtain in its fully extended position so that it dries off more quickly. Some bathrooms have hotlights which light and heat the room while you bathe or shower. *showers*

These can be very well appointed indeed and may be full of amazing electric gadgets, such as electric carving knives — which are good fun but perhaps a little dangerous. **kitchens**

Most Americans do not possess an electric kettle. This means that water has to be heated up in all sorts of slow, laborious and archaic ways, such as in a saucepan. (If you just want to heat up a cup of water, it can be done in a microwave oven, if there is one.)

Many American homes do not have a tea-pot. Regrettably, tea in that case has often to be made by the tea-bag-in-the-cup method. (It is also possible to make tea in some automatic coffee-makers.)

In many urban areas where water supplies are polluted and heavily chlorinated, kitchen cold-water taps may be fitted with filters that you turn on if you are going to drink the water rather than wash something with it.

Cookers normally do not have grills. Instead they have 'broilers', which are basically the same thing, except that they are larger (to accommodate those enormous steaks), are located in or below the oven and have no temperature control. There are several disadvantages to this: you cannot bake or roast and grill at the same time (unless you have a double-oven cooker); you have to grill at a single heat; and if you want toast, you have to use a toaster or else the special small, portable grill oven that is also frequently found in American kitchens. (These grill ovens are also useful for heating up frozen foods — if there isn't a microwave.) *cookers*

Americans do not normally warm plates before serving food on them, and there is therefore no provision for this on their cookers.

disposing of
rubbish

Americans often make a distinction between two different types of rubbish (and they do produce enormous quantities of both sorts). 'Trash' refers to paper, glass and tin, while 'garbage' means animal and vegetable matter. Many kitchens have garbage-disposal units. You empty the garbage into the sink, switch on the unit, run the cold water, and it disappears. A good unit will handle anything up to chicken bones.

Some places, particularly apartments, have 'trash compacters'. These are rubbish bins that incorporate a unit that you can switch on to crush and squash the rubbish to make for convenience in disposing of it.

cellars

Many American houses have cellars. These are very useful for storing things in, for keeping cool in hot weather and for sheltering from tornadoes (see page 17).

pest control

The climate and the range of insect life found in America mean that homes in many areas are much more prone than those in Europe to infestation by things like cockroaches and even termites. Many households, therefore, have regular visits from pest-control agencies, who spray bathrooms, kitchens and other susceptible areas.

swimming
pools and
'hot tubs'

In many parts of the country it is not at all uncommon for middle-class households to have a swimming pool. These are sometimes heated, sometimes not. If you find yourself in charge of a house with a pool, remember that it needs looking after. It has to be cleaned, filtered, filled, chlorinated, etc. – which all costs money, of course. There are firms that specialize in calling at your house and doing these things for you if you prefer.

The 'hot tub' is a particularly, but not exclusively, Californian phenomenon. It is located in the garden (US: yard) if the climate permits and generally consists of a large, circular, wooden tub containing continuously hot water, together with devices for keeping the water hot. You sit in it. Why do you sit in it? Well, it's very relaxing; your bathroom bathtub isn't half as comfortable (see above); you can sit and look at the stars at night; the water never gets cold; and it's big enough for

several people to sit in at once. In other words, you don't
wash in it, you socialize — and, yes, you are supposed
to take all your clothes off (but only if everyone else
does).

The ideal temperature is said by some to be about
104 °F (40 °C), but do make sure that the water is not
too hot for you. Don't stay in too long, especially if
you're drunk — people have been known to faint and
drown.

A 'jacuzzi' is a similar affair, but rather more bubbly.

TV and Radio

television American television has the reputation of being terrible. It is. You will, from time to time, find good programmes (US: shows), but many of these are imported from Britain or elsewhere. TV reception, too, is often not very good. Many Americans do not have an outside aerial (US: antenna), and American sets work on a different system from the one used in Europe and do not give such a sharp or clear picture.

The main function of most American TV is to make money. The more popular the programme, the more advertising revenue it will attract and everything is therefore done to make most programmes as popular as possible. TV programmes are advertised in advance almost as much as washing powders — and *during* other programmes as well as between them. And if a programme does not get a sufficiently high audience rating, it is dropped more or less instantly. You will appreciate, therefore, that very little time is devoted, at least on the main networks, to minority interests. You should not expect to find programmes on chess, bee keeping or the learning of German.

networks and In the USA there is no national television as such. There
stations are three main national networks: ABC, CBS and NBC. These networks have hundreds of 'affiliated stations' — local stations that are attached to one network and take its programmes, rather in the way that British pubs are attached to one brewery and take its beers. The local stations also show their own local news, sport and other broadcasts, and these are often astonishingly amateurish. There are also independent stations (like Free Houses, to continue with the brewing analogy), but these are often confined to showing old programmes or films or to specializing in some other way.

Hardly anything is shown live, apart from local news and discussions and major sporting events. Most programmes are taped to allow for showing at different times in the different time zones (see page 14) or even to allow

'*The trouble is not in your set — the President actually said that.*'

From the *Saturday Review*

local stations to show them at times that suit them best. The local stations can switch from local to nationally networked programmes and back again, and this may on occasion lead to an infuriating practice: a station may announce 'We will now join a show already in progress' (who wants to see half a programme?)

In addition to the networks there is the Public Broadcasting System (PBS), which operates in a similar manner to the networks but is not commercially based. Instead the PBS stations receive donations from the Government, the public, foundations and businesses. It is on the PBS stations that you will encounter most imported and high-quality programmes. (There are some parts of the country that do not have a PBS station.)

In the large cities you may have as many as twenty channels to choose from. In smaller towns and rural areas there may be only three. Very many areas, though, have now acquired 'cable TV'. In these areas you can rent a device giving you access to a large number of channels, with stations being 'piped in' from other areas, and many other facilities: weather information, twenty-four hour sports broadcasts, uncut films, pop videos etc.

American TV sets have two selector knobs. One gives you channels 1 to 13 (usually for the major network stations) and also has a UHF position. This position gives you access to the UHF stations, which you tune into (and there may be over sixty positions you can switch to) by using the second knob.

commercials PBS stations do not have commercials. This does not necessarily mean, however, that they operate just like BBC TV. Unfortunately, PBS stations sometimes interrupt programmes to advertise *themselves* by giving details of future programmes or making requests for donations. And from time to time they also have to devote whole days, or even a week, to appealing to the public to send them money.

All the other stations are intensely commercial. You may be used to advertising on European TV, but this is no preparation for coping with advertising on American television, which is loud, unsubtle, mostly unamusing and incredibly frequent (up to 14 minutes an hour). There is little, and rather weak, legislation covering the frequency of advertising and the use of 'natural breaks'. It is thus not impossible for a half-hour programme to be interrupted as many as four or five times. One never really gets used to this, and it is intensely irritating at first. Particularly obnoxious is the practice of showing commercials relatively infrequently at the beginning of a film and *very* frequently at the end, when viewers are caught up in the story.

Adverts are often inserted immediately after the opening credits of a programme and immediately before the closing credits, rather than between programmes. There is also no real warning that commercials are on their way — they just start. You get used to this in time, but it is sometimes difficult at first to tell what is advert and what is programme.

At election time there is also an astonishing amount of political advertising on TV. Politicians are not limited to party political broadcasts of a certain length, as they are in Britain and elsewhere, and can buy as much advertising time as they have money for. And they do have to pay for the advertising. There is no system of free access to TV for political parties.

films Nearly all programmes on American TV last for half an hour or multiples of half an hour. There is no such thing as a fifty-minute or a seventy-minute show. This, of course, makes the co-ordination of stations and advertising simpler. It also, however, means that dreadful things have to be done to cinema films to make them the right length. Large bits may be hacked out, or they may be padded out with advertising, though some cinema films, apparently, are now constructed so that they can later be shown on TV without too much deformation.

Most stations show game shows and chat shows in the morning; game shows, soap operas and old movies in the afternoon; and game shows, police dramas, situation comedies and chat shows in the evening. Saturday mornings are devoted to cartoons and children's programmes.   *programmes*

Game shows are like the quizzes and competitions that you find on British television but are generally a good deal worse. Colossal prizes are awarded for very little effort; audiences sound as if they are frothing at the mouth; and participants jump up and down and applaud themselves like chimpanzees.

News coverage is inadequate. The independent stations, for the most part, show only local news, and the network channels have only one major news broadcast each per evening. These main news programmes currently last for thirty minutes, of which nearly ten minutes is advertising, so there is very little time for in-depth treatment. Coverage of foreign news is very meagre, except on PBS, and current affairs programmes and discussions are rare. For weather reports, see page 17.

Sports coverage of individual games (other than soccer, see page 117) is excellent, but sports news in general, except for local news, is inadequately covered.

Do not expect to see uncut films on American network TV. The networks do not permit nudity — not even naked breasts, and not even late at night (PBS does). Neither do they permit swearing. It is OK, apparently, to say 'damn' on network TV, but you cannot say 'goddam'. Swearing is not, of course, a 'problem' in programmes written for TV, but 'difficulties' do arise with cinema films and unscripted dialogue. (Drama is no problem because there isn't any.) The solution to the 'problem' is to bleep out any swearing. You will therefore hear people in chat shows saying things like 'BLEEP-damn'. (Cable TV however, is something else. Here anything goes on some of the stations.) Networks also even stoop to the ridiculous practice of bleeping out the names of the other networks.   *censorship*

Evangelical protestantism (see page 110) is a force it is   *religious TV* hard to ignore in the USA even if you want to (and even devout foreign Christians probably will). Unfortunately, this force extends into television. There are twenty-four-hour-a-day religious stations available on cable TV, and even ordinary stations are quite liable to show programmes such as *The PTL Club* (PTL stands for 'Praise the Lord'). These programmes are concerned with sin and salvation: if you send them money, they will pray for you. Very many Americans watch these broadcasts, but foreign visitors of whatever religious persuasion seem unanimous in being amazed and appalled at this phenomenon.

radio   American radio is really excellent if you want to listen to music, but, except for the PBS stations ('National Public Radio'), there is relatively little in the way of news, talks, current affairs or drama. (For weather reports, see page 17.)

There are two bands on American radio sets. The FM band is the same as VHF, while the AM band corresponds to medium wave. The FM band extends from 88 to 108 on the dial. The VHF band on many British radios extends only from 88 to 101, so they are unable to pick up many of the American stations.

Like TV, radio is very local, only more so. If you are driving around the country, you may find you have to tune in to a new station every 50 miles (80 kilometres) or so. News reports are often taken from national networks, but most other programming is local. Most stations broadcast on either AM or FM, not both. AM stations tend to be 'top forty' stations (not too dissimilar from BBC Radio 1), or Country and Western, or 'easy listening', plus sport. FM stations tend to specialize in playing rock albums, Country and Western, soul music, classical music, etc. You will almost certainly be able to find a station you like. And the advertising is a good deal less obtrusive than it is on TV.

The radio stations are hard to distinguish between at first because they all have unmemorable letter-names, such as 'WLS' or 'KQED'.

Quaint Institutions and Customs

There are many American customs, ways, habits and institutions that are different from those elsewhere. Here are some that it can be useful for the visitor to know about.

Americans often use terms associated with their educational system assuming that foreigners will understand what they mean, which is not always the case. When you are in the USA you frequently hear people saying things like 'He's a junior in high school', 'When I was a sophomore . . .', 'They're in fourth grade', and so on.

the educational system

Americans start school when they are 6. (Children younger than that are called 'pre-schoolers' and may attend nursery school or kindergarten.) Their first year is known as 'first grade' and each year, all being well, they go up a grade until they leave school at age 18, from twelfth grade. Thus if you want to know how old children are when you hear these 'grade' terms used, you add 5 or 6 to the number of the grade. Fourth-graders, for instance, are normally 9 or 10 years old.

Education systems vary from place to place, but typically 'grade school' or 'elementary school' means first to sixth, seventh or eighth grade, 'junior high school' covers seventh, eighth and sometimes ninth grade, and 'high school' goes from ninth or tenth to twelfth grade.

Schoolchildren are often referred to as 'students'.

In high school the following terms are used:

high school

freshman	14—15 years	first year	ninth grade
sophomore	15—16 years	second year	tenth grade
junior	16—17 years	third year	eleventh grade
senior	17—18 years	fourth year	twelfth grade

In many parts of the USA, high schools are very important social centres. They are not just places that you leave at 4 p.m. and forget all about till next day.

Participation in and spectatorship at school sports events in particular are central, and all the paraphernalia that goes along with college sport (see below and page 113) is also found at the high-school level.

High schools are also important centres for events such as dances — including formal dances known as 'proms' — and teenage culture in many areas focuses on activities associated with the school.

college After leaving high school, a relatively high proportion of American children go to 'college'. This label is used both for places actually called 'colleges' and for undergraduate study at universities. Colleges and universities can also be referred to as 'schools'.

The terms 'freshman', 'sophomore', 'junior' and 'senior' are also used for the four years of undergraduate study leading to bachelors' degrees. 'Coed' is an abbreviation for 'co-educational' but, strangely enough, is also used to mean a female college student.

Americans are very sentimental about their institutions, as they are also about their flag and their country (see below). This is demonstrated in their attitudes to their schools and colleges. Colleges and universities devote considerable attention to their 'alumni' (former students), who are strongly encouraged to keep in touch with their 'alma mater' — and to send it money. And colleges even have yearly events called 'homecomings': alumni are supposed to return to the college and take part in various activities. ('Homecomings' are aped by many schools.) There are also, at some places, other bizarre annual events such as 'fathers' day', 'siblings weekend', etc. These are often linked with sports events.

graduation In the USA you graduate not only from university but also from high school and even sometimes from junior high school. At schools and colleges alike, there are ceremonies to celebrate graduation, complete with caps, gowns, diplomas and speeches by staff and students. (Oddly enough, these ceremonies, which naturally come at the end of the school or college year, are often known as 'commencement'.) It is a particular honour for a student to be appointed 'valedictorian', the person who delivers the farewell speech. This is usually the top student in the class.

(There are reports of graduation ceremonies taking

place in grade schools and even kindergartens. This book prefers not to believe them.)

If you have any connection with American colleges and universities, you will come across a number of strange phenomena. Strangest of all are the peculiarly American institutions called 'fraternities' and 'sororities'. These are nationwide institutions named with Greek letters (for example, Chi Omega). The system is therefore sometimes known as the 'Greek system'. Fraternities and sororities have houses on or near campuses where students live. The percentage of students living in fraternity and sorority houses varies widely from campus to campus.

fraternities and sororities

As the names suggest, fraternities and sororities are single-sex institutions, and each of them tends to specialize in catering for students from a particular type of social background and in cultivating a particular type of ethos. They can be somewhat snobbish and may operate as 'old-boy networks' after the students leave college (cf. British public schools).

In order to join a fraternity or sorority on a particular campus, freshmen have to be accepted into it by the students who are already members. Freshmen attend 'rush' parties to see if they like and are liked by the members. If a student is accepted, he or she becomes a 'pledge' and often has to do all sorts of silly things before moving into the house as a sophomore to join the 'brothers' or 'sisters'. Fraternities also have very sexist-sounding appendages called 'little sisters', women students who are linked to the fraternity and who can be called upon to attend parties, arrange flowers and sew on buttons — or something like that.

There is a lot more to the Greek system than this, but one would have to be an anthropologist to provide a thorough analysis. Various explanations have been given for the rise of these bodies in America, but it may, in part, be a response by students to being on enormous campuses (some universities have more than 30,000 students). As to the question of why anyone should want to join a single-sex institution with a Greek name so badly that they are prepared to go through initiation ceremonies of amazing silliness and humiliation — this is probably something that no outsider is qualified to answer. (Perhaps, though, the products of certain British public schools might have some idea.)

American laws and regulations

gambling

In most areas of the USA gambling is not allowed, so don't expect to find casinos or even betting offices. In fact, official American attitudes to gambling are very puritanical (cf. alcohol, page 73). Unofficial attitudes are something else; there is, for example, a lot of informal and undercover gambling on American football results. In some areas, though, gambling is permitted. This is notoriously true of Nevada, with its big gambling centres of Las Vegas and Reno. Las Vegas, in fact, really only exists as it does because of the anti-gambling laws in other states. More recently, Atlantic City, New Jersey, has also become a gambling centre.

Note that what is known in British English as a 'fruit machine' is called a 'slot machine' or simply a 'slot'.

Lotteries are found in many areas, and legal on-track betting takes place at horse races. (Off-track betting is illegal in most places.)

sex

There are lots of strange sex laws on the books of the American states, and in certain parts of the country, especially parts of the South and Midwest, attitudes can be very puritanical. (In other areas, especially in some of the big cities, attitudes are very liberal.) The only law likely to be of concern to visitors is that concerning the age of consent. This varies from state to state but is usually higher than 16. The age of 18 is not unusual. 'Statutory' rape is a peculiarly American crime and means the breaking of the age-of-consent laws. In some states it is actually treated as if it really were rape.

In San Francisco and New York City attitudes towards gays are much more liberal and open than they are in most European cities. In some other areas of the USA the reverse is true.

the American flag

The American flag is an entirely different order of object from the flags of Western European countries. It is a sacred object, which must not be left in the dark, must not get wet and must not touch the ground. And you certainly cannot make shopping bags or underpants out of it. Until recently, in fact, American schoolchildren had to say a pledge of allegiance *to the flag* every day — really! (In some places the practice still continues.) A good rule of thumb is that the American flag is very like HM the Queen of England — it is treated with the same amount of respect.

You will probably already know what the American flag looks like, but if you don't, you will have plenty of opportunity to find out while you are in the USA. The flag is paraded at all sporting events, including high school games, and is flown over all Government offices — which is helpful if you're looking for the post office. Other places also fly it, including restaurants. But wherever you see it, it is probably impolite to make jokes about it and certainly inadvisable.

Americans can be noisily and embarrassingly patriotic. (Europeans, of course, generally feel proud of their countries too, but, except at sporting events, they tend to keep it more to themselves than Americans do.) America, moreover, is not a country but a *nation*, even when it comes to weather forecasts, and politicians and advertisers keep reminding everybody of what a wonderful nation it is. (In many respects they are quite right, of course — you just wish they wouldn't keep on *saying* so.) Advertisers, too, like to call their audience 'America', as in 'Hi there, America!'

patriotism

There are four main national holidays (as opposed to vacations — note that Americans say *holiday* only for these public commemorations):

national holidays and other occasions

Memorial Day	Falls on the last Monday in May. Commemorates the Americans who have died in wars. Leads to a long holiday weekend that signals the start of summer.
Fourth of July	Anniversary of the USA's independence from Britain. Celebrated with picnics and fireworks (except that fireworks are illegal in many places, apart from those organized for public display).
Labor Day	Falls on the first Monday in September and marks the end of summer. Supposed to honour the American worker, and an important holiday for many trade unions.
Thanksgiving	Celebrated on the fourth Thursday in November. Commemorates the first harvest of European settlers. The whole family gets together and eats turkey,

stuffing, cranberry sauce and pumpkin pie.

Mother's Day is the second Sunday in May (i.e. not the same as in Britain), and Fathers' Day is the third Sunday in June. The American card companies have also invented Grandparents' Day and Mother-in-Laws' Day.

Hallowe'en (31 October) is celebrated by children throughout the USA and if they knock at your door that evening (often dressed up in costumes), you are expected to give them sweets or other gifts.

There are many other local and national days and holidays. Government holidays, when institutions such as post offices may be closed, include Presidents' Day (in February), Columbus Day (12 October) and Veterans' Day (11 November).

religion   Fundamentalist, evangelical Protestantism is something most foreigners are not used to and something you cannot escape in the USA, especially in the South and Midwest. It is clearly a force to be reckoned with in American society and politics, and you come across it on the radio and TV (see page 103) and also in the form of advertisements and bumper stickers.

It is quite entertaining, at first, to listen to the preachers ranting and raving, but it has to be appreciated that they are *perfectly serious*. Indeed, there are large numbers of people in the USA, some of them very influential, who genuinely believe that the Book of Genesis is literally true and that Darwin's or *any* theory of evolution is nonsense. In fact, they believe that the whole Bible is literally true.

Even ordinary Christianity is a much more prominent feature of American life than it is in most parts of Northern Europe or Australia. Many more Americans go to church, and many American politicians, sportsmen and public figures have no qualms about calling on God in public or about talking about their private religious beliefs in front of millions of TV viewers. And it seems to be a lot more common, too, for Americans to say grace before meals.

In spite of the high visibility of Protestantism in America, there is a huge variety of other religious groups, some of which (e.g. Jews and Roman Catholics) are politically influential locally or nationally. (Note that, perhaps as a consequence of this, Americans say 'first name' or 'given name' rather than 'Christian name'.)

If you want to find a church to attend in the USA, you can easily locate the one of your choice in the telephone Yellow Pages.

Until recently American newspapers were nearly all local papers, with *Time* and *Newsweek* filling the gap. Nowadays, however, satellite technology means that, for example, the *New York Times* is becoming more and more available in other parts of the country, as is also the newly founded *US Today*, which can be found in most urban areas from late morning onwards. The *Wall Street Journal, Christian Science Monitor*, and *Los Angeles Times* are also widely available.

American newspapers are extremely thick and heavy, but they do not, in most cases, actually contain any more reading matter than European papers — it's all advertising.

newspapers

If you have a residence in the USA, you can have newspapers delivered. Note, however, that in some places you order papers not through a newsagent but direct from the newspaper company — and each different paper you have delivered will be brought by a different paper boy or girl. (And these kids really do *throw* the paper on to your lawn or driveway. They are supposed to put it in a polythene cover if it is raining.) In other places you do place your order through a newsagent.

having your paper delivered

Films in the USA are graded as follows:

cinema

classification of films

G   unrestricted — anyone can see it
PG   unrestricted but 'parental guidance' is recommended
R   restricted to people over a certain age (often 18) or people younger than that accompanied by a parent or guardian
X   restricted to people over a certain age (often 18).

A very American institution is the outdoor drive-in movie theatre. At these places you pay as you enter, park your car in a marked space and sit in the car and watch the film (or pretend to). You listen to the soundtrack through a small loudspeaker, which is wired to a stand and which you hang in through the car window. Don't forget to

drive-in movies

remove the loudspeaker before you drive off afterwards.

Obviously, drive-in movie theatres only operate after dark, and only in the summer in the colder areas. They do not normally show the very latest or best films — probably because most people go to drive-ins to do things other than watch the film.

beaches   America has thousands of miles of coastline, but it is actually surprisingly difficult to get down to the sea (Americans say the 'ocean'). In many areas there are off-shore bars, islands, swamps or cliffs that block access to the open sea. And in other areas there are actually private beaches — in some states there is no notion that the shore should belong to everyone.

Typically, Americans do not dress and undress on the beach, and they may stare at you if you do. (On some Eastern beaches, in fact, it is actually illegal.) Neither is it very often that you see topless sunbathing on American beaches as yet. Beaches also tend to be a good deal more 'organized' than those in many parts of Europe: they are often liberally supplied with lifeguards, and have closing times, a bit like British pubs.

For sharks, see page 19.

showers   Wedding 'showers' and baby 'showers' are get-togethers organized by women, at which a woman who is about to get married or have a baby is given appropriate presents. Light refreshments are consumed and games are some-times played. They are also sometimes organized on a 'surprise' basis.

Watching and Understanding Sport

In the USA sport is known as 'sports' and is a branch of show business, as you will observe if you watch matches (US: games) live or on TV. Professional sport is also very *big* business. Teams are supposed to make money for their owners, and there is very little room in the USA for the Hartlepools and Wigans of the sporting world. There is also relatively little local loyalty at the top level – if a club is losing money in Oakland, the owner will simply move it (or try to move it) to Los Angeles, players, coaches and all, though actual supporters (US: fans) are just as loyal as supporters anywhere else.

College sport is also extremely important in the USA (universities actually award *scholarships* to good players). And in basketball and American football, playing for a college team is a normal preliminary to becoming a professional player. (In ice hockey, a normal preliminary to becoming a professional is being a Canadian.)

The main professional sports are American football (known as 'football'), which is played in the autumn and early winter; ice hockey (known as 'hockey') and basketball, which are played in the winter and spring; and baseball, which is played in the spring and summer.

American sport, at the professional level, is dominated by television. In addition to normal 'time-outs' (see below), games being televised are subject to 'officials' time-outs', which are simply breaks to permit the showing of commercials. And the presentation of trophies to winning teams is often done in dressing-rooms, out of sight of the crowd, so that TV cameras and close-up microphones can be present.

Americans do not often have the pleasure, as football- and cricket-playing nations do, of seeing their national teams competing against other countries. American football is played only in America (except that Canadian football is very similar); baseball is mostly, though by no means exclusively, an American, Canadian and Japanese game; ice hockey in the USA is played mostly by Cana-

dians and other foreigners; and basketball outside the
USA is played mostly by amateurs, whereas the best
Americans are professionals.

This does not, however, prevent Americans from
using terms like 'world champion'. The winners of the
American football league are referred to, with amazing
immodesty, as the 'world champions'. (Strictly speaking,
this is true, of course — they are the world champions at
American football.) And the baseball finals are known as
the 'World Series'. Just try not to let this bother you.
One day America may be very good at soccer, and then
they may have real world champions.

going to a game Be warned that before *every* sporting event, however
small and unimportant it is, the American flag is paraded,
and the American national anthem is not only played
but also sung. (If you ask Americans *why* this is, they
have no idea.) This custom is very tedious. However,
you *are* supposed to stand up when this happens, and
you will even see some people placing their right hands
on the left side of their chests. This has to do with the
location of their hearts (for more on patriotism and the
American flag, see page 108).

crowd stimulants The show-business side of American sport is particularly
apparent in the use of 'cheerleaders'. In the case of
college sport these are generally athletic young women
and men who perform various acrobatic feats and attempt
to get the crowd to cheer and support their team. Crowds
often seem unable to do this of their own accord and are
generally most unimaginative about what they do chant
and shout. 'Go, Reds, beat Blues!' is not untypical. At
professional matches the cheerleaders are usually scantily
dressed and not particularly athletic young women who
(supposedly) perform the same function.

College football is also notable for the presence of
marching bands, composed of students, who play before
the match and at half-time. They look rather military
and have nothing whatsoever to do with the football,
but they are sometimes very good. Bands also play at
college basketball games (often while the game is actually
in progress, believe it or not), in order to stimulate the
crowd. Baseball games, on the other hand, are plagued
by electric organs, which also play while the game is in
progress.

Drawing by Ziegler; © 1984 The New Yorker Magazine, Inc.

You will have to get used to the vocal antics of American sports crowds. They don't normally chant obscene verses in unison, as fans do at British football matches, but they do scream, shriek and go in for falsetto whoops. You may see American fans, particularly in front of TV cameras, holding their forefingers up in the air. This means '(Our team is) *number one*', i.e. the best.

the crowd

If you have paid for admission to a baseball game and the game is rained off, your ticket will become valid as a 'rain check', giving you admission to another game (hence the American expression 'I'll take a rain check on that').

cancelled games

Sports teams are usually singular in American English (unless they have a plural name like 'The Kicks'). Reports of British football matches say things like: 'Arsenal has won the cup', 'West Ham is winning', 'Liverpool, which is the champion . . .', 'Everton has scored its second goal.' People aren't particularly consistent, though, since you'll often hear things like 'Detroit is winning, aren't they?'

    The manager of a team is called the 'coach' (and may even be addressed and referred to as, e.g., 'Coach Smith'), except in baseball, where he is called the manager.

    The referees, linesmen, umpires, etc. are referred to as 'officials'.

    Players are often called 'athletes' even when, as is the case with the larger American football players, they look most unathletic.

sports language

team members and officials

some common　Americans play 'on' a team, not 'in' one.
terms　　　　Attack and defence are called, respectively, 'OFFense' and 'DEfense'.

A 'rookie' is a player in his first year.

If a game is 'called', it is called off.

If a game is 'tied up', this simply means that the scores are level.

'In the clutch' means 'at a crucial point in the game'.

To 'second guess' means to have second thoughts about some tactic etc. after the event; it can also mean to outguess someone.

The 'MVP' is the 'most valuable player', i.e. the man of the match or something similar.

'Co-ed' sport simply means 'mixed' (male and female).

'Time out': American football and basketball both permit a number of 'time-outs' during a match when one of the sides can elect to stop the game for a short time while they discuss tactics or, in football, save time between plays (see below).

'A foul on Smith' means that Smith has *committed* a foul, and that a foul (i.e. penalty, etc.) has been awarded *against* him.

'Overtime' means extra time.

'Astroturf' is artificial grass.

'halls of fame'　Several sports have a 'hall of fame'. These are museum-type places devoted to a particular sport, and especially good players are 'elected' to the 'hall of fame', where exhibits are devoted to them.

fixtures and　In fixtures and results the home team is often given
results　　　second, the away team first. Thus 'Los Angeles *v.* San Francisco' means that the match is to be in San Francisco and is often read as 'Los Angeles at San Francisco'. The away team is often said to be 'on the road'.

Sports commentators and writers don't like giving you the results clearly and simply by saying, for example, 'Arsenal 2, Tottenham 1'. Instead, they search for vivid synonyms for 'beat', which means that you, the listener or reader, have to concentrate hard to understand what is going on. Here are some American soccer results from the *Chicago Sun-Times*:

The Atlanta Chiefs beat the Portland Timber 2—1,
the Washington Diplomats beat the Philadelphia

Fury 2—1, the Cosmos trimmed the New England Tea Men 2—1, the California Surf blanked the Minnesota Kicks 1—0, the Rochester Lancers nipped the San Jose Earthquakes 2—1, and the San Diego Sockers shut out the Vancouver Whitecaps 1—0.

The letter F by a result means 'final', i.e. final score. 'Zip' and 'zilch' means 'zero'. '2—1', etc. is not read as '2—1' but as '2 to 1'. 'San Diego is 4—0' is read as 'San Diego is four and oh' and means that San Diego have won four matches and lost none. 'Portland is 4 of 6' or '4 for 6' means they have won four matches out of six.

soccer

A good way of getting a feel for the nature of sport in the USA is to look at the playing and reporting of a game familiar to most Europeans, namely football. This is known as 'soccer' in the USA to distinguish it from American football and is increasingly being played in schools, in colleges and professionally.

Most indigenous American sports require you to be extremely tall, strong, heavy, or all three — which means that most people are excluded from top-level play. (Players' heights and weights are often listed with their names in programmes.) The advantage of football, as Americans are now beginning to realize, is that all it requires is skill and fitness, and many more people can therefore take part. (And it doesn't require lots of expensive equipment either.)

In Britain football has a somewhat robust, proletarian kind of image. In America, on the other hand — except amongst people of Mexican or recent immigrant origins — football is a rather intellectual, middle-class kind of activity, and is especially popular amongst women.

TV coverage

TV coverage of soccer is infrequent and varies from bad to atrocious. The cameramen do well with a game that is unfamiliar to many of them, but the producers and commentators do not. Their worst problem is a failure to recognize that football is a game of continuous action — commercials are actually shown and sideline interviews conducted *while play is in progress*. This is infuriating.

the pitch   Many football matches are played on astroturf pitches designed for American football. Others are played on baseball pitches, which are not entirely covered by grass. In both cases the surface is not ideal and play suffers.

interpreting   American sport (like other aspects of American life,
press reports   notably weather reporting) is obsessed with statistics. This obsession has found its way into the coverage of football. For example, goalkeepers (nearly always known as 'goalies') are ranked according to the number of their 'shut-outs' — games in which they have not conceded a goal — and according to the average number of goals that they have let in per match, which, of course, ignores the fact that it is the defence as a whole that is responsible for these figures.

Americans have also invented something called an 'assist'; a player who passes the ball to another, who then scores, is credited with an assist. In the ranking of goal scorers, one point is awarded to a player for an assist, two for a goal.

The following is a typical piece of American soccer reporting. This extract is from the *San Francisco Chronicle*. It gives you plenty of figures but very little else and is indicative of this statistical way of looking at sport:

BEST'S GOAL GIVES QUAKES
FIRST VICTORY

The San Jose Earthquakes won their first North American Soccer League game of the year last night at Spartan Stadium, defeating the Edmonton Drillers, 1—0.

A crowd of 10,763 looked on as the Quakes reaped the benefits of signing soccer superstar George Best.

Best looked like the game's goat when he missed a penalty kick in the 74th minute. But he more than made up for it five minutes later, when the recently-acquired English [sic] star fed Steve David and David scored the only goal of the game with 10:20 remaining.

Quakes goalie Mike Hewitt had to turn aside only four shots, while San Jose took 19 shots at busy Edmonton goalie Peritti Alaja.

The rough contest saw 72 fouls called and Mike

Czuczman of San Jose ejected with five minutes left, but even playing one man short, San Jose dominated the offense.

The Earthquakes are now 1—6 this season, and entrenched in last place in the NASL's American Conference West. Edmonton is 3—4.

San Jose will host Houston at Spartan Stadium tomorrow afternoon. The Hurricane is 2—5 after losing to Los Angeles, 3—2, last night.

The following is the result of a match between San Jose Earthquakes and Houston in San Jose, as reported in the same newspaper:

Quakes, 3—0

Houston	0	0—0
San Jose	1	2—3

First Half — 1. SJ, David 4 (Kraay, Maseko) 8:30. Cautions — Czuczman, SJ, 30:26.

Second Half — 2. SJ, David 5 (Maseko 63:09); 3. SJ, David 6 (Best) 83:56. Cautions — None.

Shots — Houston 16-8—24, San Jose 5-0—13. Saves — By Hammond (Hou) 3-2—5, By Hewitt (SJ) 5-2—7. Corners — Hou 4-5—9, SJ 4-4—8. Fouls — Hou 7-6—13, SJ 10-8—19.

Attendance — 13,118.

It tells you that San Jose won 3—0, and that they scored once in the first half, twice in the second. The first goal was scored for San Jose by David (bringing his season's total to four) from 'assists' by Kraay and Maseko, after eight and a half minutes. San Jose's Cruczman was cautioned after thirty minutes and twenty-six seconds . . . and so on. You can also see how many shots, saves, corners and fouls there were per team in each half and overall.

If you are starved of British and other European foot-ball results, you will be able to find them in *some* of the big-city newspapers (for example, those of Los Angeles, San Francisco, Cleveland, New York) on Sundays or Mondays. Short-wave radios can pick up the BBC World Service.

Professional indoor soccer is played in the USA in the winter. It is similar to, but not the same as, five-a-side football. It is played on artificial turf on ice hockey rinks *professional indoor soccer* and rebounds off the boards are used extensively. Balls above shoulder height are allowed. There are six players a side on the pitch at any one time. Thirteen out of the sixteen players that each team is allowed in a squad must be Americans. As in ice hockey, some fouls are penalized by sending players off for a specified period of time.

The commissioner of the Indoor Soccer League is quoted as saying of the game:

> We call it the Americanization of the world's most popular game. We cut down the midfield action and brought the fans closer to the game. There's more aggression, more action, more scoring. An average game will produce almost 100 shots on goal, and there are usually more than a dozen goals scored in each game.

Really — that's what he said. Enough said.

American football

Someone once described American football as a cross between rugby and World War II. It certainly is brutal and violent, and the players really need all the protective clothing they wear. But it is also a fascinating and exciting game of skill and strategy, and if you enjoy football or rugby, you will probably like it — at least, if you work a little, initially, at understanding what is happening.

There is no space here to give a full account of all the subtleties of American football. It is a very complicated game. This section merely provides a summary of its main features, so that your first match will not be too confusing. And the principles will probably not mean a great deal to you until you have actually seen at least part of a match in progress.

Your first encounter with this game, unless you are an important business executive, is quite likely to be at a college game or on TV, since the professional teams play only sixteen games a year, and many are fully sold out.

some preliminaries

Basically, American football is a rugby-type game (and, indeed, developed out of rugby), played with a rugby-shaped ball. But there are three basic differences.

1   Play is not continuous. The game is organized in a series of 'plays', and each time a player is tackled to the ground with the ball or the ball goes out of play, the 'play' is concluded.

2   One forward pass per play is permitted. This is a
     spectacular and exciting part of the game.
3   Players are allowed to block, push over or stop
     opposing players who are not in possession of the
     ball. (There *are* rules about this — you can't, for
     instance, use your hands to do it.)

The object of the game, as in rugby, is to score by
getting into the end-zone with the ball for a touch-down
(so called, although it is not, in fact, necessary to touch
the ball to the ground). The pitch is 100 yards (91.44
metres) long, and has long lines drawn across it at 5-yard
(4.57 metre) intervals, with shorter lines between them
marking every yard. A team is given up to four attempts,
called 'downs', to advance the ball a total of at least 10
yards (9.14 metres). If it succeeds in doing this, it gets
four more attempts for another 10 yards, and so on. If
it fails, the other team wins possession of the ball at the
point reached by the offense, though this does not
usually happen (see below).

There are eleven men per side on the field at any one
time, but professional clubs have completely separate
offensive and defensive teams, and extensive and continuous substitution and resubstitution are normal.

Games last one hour on the clock. This time is divided
up into four quarters, with a break after the second
quarter. However, since the clock runs only when play is
actually in progress, a game, including half-time, may
last nearly three hours (and longer if overtime is needed
to break a tie).

At the beginning of each play the offense (the team with   *tactics and*
the ball) groups in a 'huddle', where the forthcoming   *strategy*
play is announced or planned. Then most of the players
in each team line up, facing each other, at the 'line of
scrimmage'. The offensive 'center', who stands in the
middle of the line, 'snaps' the ball back through his legs
to the 'quarter-back', who is standing behind him. The
quarter-back then (usually) drops back a few yards. The
defensive team often tries to break through the offensive
line to get at the quarter-back and stop him getting rid
of the ball. If the defense succeeds, the move is called a
'sack'. Most often they don't, however, and the quarter-
back makes a play in one of three ways.

1   He can give or pass the ball to a 'running back' who
    has also been standing behind the line, who will try
    to run the ball up the field, avoiding tackles by the
    defense. Running in front of the running back will
    often be players from his own team, who try to
    block defensive players from tackling him. Usually
    the back is tackled to the ground, sometimes with-
    out having made much progress at all, or he is pushed
    into touch, at which point the play ends. The next
    play begins level with the point at which the previous
    one ended.

2   He can throw a forward pass down the field to a pass
    receiver who, at the snap, has run down the field to
    a pre-arranged position. If the receiver catches the
    ball, the pass is 'complete', and he is free to run
    with it until tackled. If he drops or misses the ball,
    the pass is 'incomplete', the play is over and no
    progress is made. Sometimes the defense succeeds
    in catching the ball instead. This is called an 'inter-
    ception', and the defense now becomes the offense,
    running back with the ball until tackled.

3   He can run with the ball himself.

Sometimes a player will 'fumble', accidentally dropping the ball and allowing the other side the possibility
of gaining possession.

There are very few 'lateral' passes of the rugby type
because of the risk of interceptions, and hardly any use
is made of the feet.

A crucial part of offensive strategy is to keep the
defense guessing about what the offense is going to do.
Players therefore sometimes *pretend* to have the ball,
and this ruse, combined with the way in which everybody seems to be tackling everybody, makes it very
confusing for beginners to work out what exactly is
happening.

In football terminology, 'second and 3' means that it
is 'second down' and 3 yards are required (to make the
10 yards). If it is 'fourth and 1' ('fourth down' with 1
yard needed), the offense may 'go for it' — try to get
the extra yard by a normal play, as described above.
But often — and certainly if it's, say, 'fourth and 8' —
the offense will not risk failing to get the extra yardage
and thereby having to give the ball to the other side. If
it is near to the opposing goal, the offense therefore
brings on a specialist kicker to try and score a 'field

goal'. At the snap, the center throws the ball back to a player who places it on the ground, so that the kicker can try and kick it between the posts, as in rugby. If the goal is too far away for a field goal attempt, a specialist 'punter' is brought on. He catches the ball from the center and drop-kicks it as far down the field as he can. The opposing team will catch it and try and run it back as far as possible before being tackled.

After a touch-down there is an attempt at a conversion, as in rugby, which proceeds as for a field goal.

You will encounter statistics as follows: *statistics*

1   for running backs: yards 'rushing' (i.e. how many yards they have gained for the team per game or per season) and the average number of yards they have gained per 'carry';
2   for quarter-backs: the percentage of passes that have been completed, the number of yards gained by successful passes, and the number of yards 'rushing';
3   for kickers: the average length of kick and the longest kick.

A good book for the beginning spectator is *Football*   *further*
Talk by Howard Liss (New York: Pocket Books).   *information*

If you like cricket, you will probably like baseball, but   **baseball**
baseball is a faster game and even non-cricket lovers may take to it. It is useful for the English, the Australians, and other truly civilized people to compare the two games, since in some respects they are similar and are founded on similar principles, though the terminology often differs. The batsman is known as the 'batter', for example; an innings is called an 'inning'; being in or batting is known as being 'at bat'; the equivalent of bowler is 'pitcher'; wicket-keeper corresponds to 'catcher'.

If you do want to watch some baseball, you will find this quite easy, since, like cricket, the game is played on most days of the week.

If you do go to a game, note that when the ball goes into the crowd, it is not thrown back. The ball is not a sacred object, as in cricket, and it is relatively cheap. Baseballs are made in that not very wealthy country, Haiti.

how the game
is played

Basically, baseball is the same as rounders, the object being to score by running round three bases and back to home base, known in baseball as 'home plate'.

Each match has nine innings, the away team always going in first in each inning. Each team has three 'outs' (cf. wickets) per inning. There are nine players in a team, and each man bats in turn, normally batting between three and five times per match. (Batters who get 'on base' — see below — are not out, which is why you can have more than three batters per inning.) In the American League, one of the two baseball leagues, pitchers do not have to bat, and specialist batters called 'designated hitters' bat for them. In the National League pitchers do have to bat. If the score after nine innings is a tie, then further innings are played until a result is achieved.

The pitcher must throw the ball so that it passes over home plate (known also as 'the plate' when pitching is being discussed). The ball must also reach the batter at a level between his shoulder and his knee. Any pitch that *does not* meet these requirements is called a 'ball', and at a fourth ball the batter gets a free 'walk' to first base. Any pitch that *does* meet these requirements and that the batter fails to hit is called a 'strike'. The pitcher, of course, is trying to throw strikes. (If the pitcher hits the batter with the ball, the batter gets a walk.) At a third strike the batter is out. He is said to have 'struck out', and the pitcher has a 'strike-out'. Commentators say things like 'The count is two and one', meaning there have been two balls and one strike on a particular batter. (The number of balls is always given before the number of strikes.) A 'full count' is three balls and two strikes.

If the batter hits the ball, he must run. If he succeeds in getting to first base (or second or third base), he is said to be 'on base'. If a batter hits the ball and gets on base, he has a 'hit'. When a hit gets him to first base, he has got a 'single', to second base a 'double', and to third base a 'triple'. If the batter hits the ball over the fence surrounding the field, it is a 'home run' (or 'homer'), and he and anyone else who is on base automatically scores. (They do have to run around to home plate, though.)

A 'foul line' is drawn on the pitch out from home plate through the first and third bases. If the batter hits or snicks the ball behind this line, the ball is 'foul' (the opposite of foul is 'fair'), and it counts as a strike, *except* that it cannot count as a third strike, i.e. the batter cannot be out on a foul unless he is caught. (Americans do not talk of batters being 'caught' — they point out, quite logically, that it is the ball that is caught.)

In addition to striking out, a batter can also be out, as in cricket, by being caught or run out. To achieve a run-out, called a 'put-out', the fielder does not actually have to touch the ball to the 'bag' marking the base — it is enough for him to be holding the ball in his hand while touching the bag with his foot. (The batter, correspondingly, throws his bat away as he sets out to run from the plate and, to be safe, has to get to the bag, touching in with his foot or hand, before the fielder.) Alternatively, a fielder can run out a batter (now known as a 'runner') by 'tagging' him. The fielder holds the ball in his hand and touches the batter with it before he reaches base.

If a batter is caught out, runners on base can't advance to the next base until after the catch is taken. If they have started, they have to go back and start again.

Only one pitcher pitches at a time, but he can be, and very often is, changed during the course of the game. Once a pitcher has been taken off, he cannot return. Pitchers are crucial players in any match, and announcements always say who the 'starting' pitcher is going to be. Pitchers are said to 'win', 'lose' or 'save' games, and pitchers are often listed as, for example, Smith (3–2), i.e. he's won three games and lost two.

The catcher doesn't look as if he is an important player. He is. He advises the pitcher on what type of pitches to throw and is crucial in achieving run-outs and in stopping 'stolen bases' (see below).

There are lots of statistics in baseball. You may find the following explanations helpful, particularly if you are trying to understand newspaper reports.

scoring and statistics

Errors are counted officially, so that batters don't get credit for, and pitchers' averages don't suffer from, fielding errors. For each inning during a match, statistics are given for runs (R), hits (H) and errors (E).

Batters' statistics are given as follows:

for each game
ab   at bats (number of times batted)
r   runs (number of times batter got round to home plate, not necessarily of his own batting — this only happens with home runs)

h   hits (number of times batter got on base, not counting walks and errors)

rbi   runs batted in (number of runs scored off batter's hits)

cumulatively

ab   at bats

h   hits

hr   home runs

ave   number of hits divided by number of at bats.

Pitchers' statistics are given as follows:

for each game

ip   innings pitched

h   hits scored off pitcher's pitching

r   runs scored off pitcher's pitching

er   earned runs (runs scored excluding those due to errors)

bb   bases on balls (walks conceded)

so   strike-outs

cumulatively

era   earned run average (average number of earned runs conceded per nine innings).

In the league tables, or 'standings', the number of games that each team has played is not given. The figures that are given are: W (games won), L (games lost), Pct (percentage of games won) and GB (games behind — that is, how many fewer games the team has won than the leading team; in calculating this, allowance is made for the number of games that the team has played by comparison with the leading team).

baseball idiom Even if you don't follow baseball, you will need to understand a number of baseball terms that Americans use metaphorically in their everyday lives — like 'to strike out', meaning 'to fail'. Here are some other terms that may puzzle you:

bull pen	where the pitchers warm up; also refers to 'relief' pitching (i.e. the list of substitute pitchers)
bunt	tap rather than hit the ball
double play	when two players are got out at the same play
fly out	be caught out off a high hit
foul out	be caught out behind the foul line

line drive	hard, low hit
pinch hitter	substitute batter
pop-up	weak, high hit
stolen base	runner advances to the next base even though there is no hit
switch-hitter	batter who can bat both right- and left-handed.

Ice hockey and basketball are quite easy to follow and to understand without any coaching, and you may have seen them at home on TV. With both games it is a relatively simple matter to pick up the rules and finer points as you go along. (Be warned, though, that the rules of college and professional basketball differ somewhat.)

ice hockey and basketball

Being Ill and Keeping Healthy

Dr A Turner writes in *The Traveller's Health Guide* (London: Lascelles): 'When a British subject is taken ill abroad . . . he realizes what a wonderful institution the much maligned National Health Service really is.' This is especially true when the British subject is in the USA. There is no National Health Service in the USA, where in general you pay for *everything* in the field of health and medicine — and expenses can be astonishingly high.

The USA is not, of course, an entirely uncivilized country, and free medical care is provided for the elderly up to a point, and provision is also made for the poor, though the treatment they get is not as good as that given to people who pay. And you don't get free treatment *until* you are poor — they may charge you for treatment until you've got no money left and *then* treat you for free. One does hear of people who cannot afford to have artificial limbs fitted and of others who have died because they did not have funds for, say, a heart pacemaker. One hopes these stories are not true.

insurance Insurance cover that will do for visiting other foreign countries will not be adequate for the USA. It is *vital* to take out good insurance before you leave and to come home immediately, if possible, if you become seriously ill.

If you are staying in America for some considerable time, you may be lucky enough to find that your employer or college will take out insurance cover for you. If you have to take out your own cover, you will discover that many American policies will cover you for *only 80 per cent* of your medical expenses — and 20 per cent of, say, $50,000 is a lot of money. Many Americans have been bankrupted by long or serious illness, and many others are frightened of being bankrupted.

medical terminology Americans are much more up on medical terminology than the British and tend to talk about such things as 'my appendectomy/tonsillectomy' rather than saying 'When I had my appendix/tonsils out . . .'

Americans often talk about being 'sick' rather than 'ill', and to say 'I feel sick' can therefore be ambiguous. If they want to make it clear that they feel as if they are going to vomit, Americans say 'I feel nauseous'.

Some terms are used in the USA that may not be familiar to speakers of British English:

gas	wind
mucous	catarrh
(menstrual) cramps	period pains
(intestinal) cramps	stomach ache (the British say 'stomach' when they mean 'intestines' — Americans don't)
strep throat	sore throat caused by bacterial infection
mono (nucleosis)	glandular fever
jock itch	rash on or around the male sex organs

Normal body temperature is said in the USA to be 98.6 °F.

drug stores

American pharmacies, drug stores (see also page 88) and supermarkets are filled with medications for every disease and condition you can think of and quite a few that you can't. They are a hypochondriac's delight. It is, however, difficult to find soluble aspirin, other than in Alka Seltzer. Tablets containing 'acetaminophen' correspond to British tablets containing paracetamol.

consulting a doctor

If you want to see a doctor, you will have to pay. Doctors do not normally make house calls at all, and they are very likely to be unavailable on Sundays or on Wednesdays (when they are said to play golf). It is best, too, not to get ill at night, at weekends or during holidays.

If doctors prescribe drugs and medicine (US: medication) for you, you will also have to pay the full price for them at the chemist's (US: pharmacist). There seems to be a tendency for doctors to prescribe treatment, tests and medication that the patient may not really need and that would probably not be recommended in Britain. One can't help thinking that the more treatment the doctors prescribe, the more money they get, but they are also said to recommend any treatment that might

From the *Saturday Review*

conceivably be relevant because they are worried about being sued by dissatisfied patients.

If you need to find a doctor to visit, you can often find clinics listed in the Yellow Pages in the phone book.

In the American system you do not have to go through a general practitioner to get access to a specialist. You can go straight to a specialist if you wish.

going into hospital The real worry is that, while in the USA, you will be in a bad car accident or will suffer a heart attack or something similar that requires immediate 'hospitalization' (as Americans say), with no prospect of a speedy return home. If you do have to go into hospital, you can expect to be very comfortable and to receive excellent treatment, but you will have to pay for each doctor who sees you, for each anaethetist who treats you, for all your food, for all your drugs and medicines, for any blood you need, for any anaesthetic used on you, and for your room. Your room may well be more expensive than a hotel room, and you can pay even more if you want a 'private' (single) or 'semi-private' (double) room, a TV set or a telephone. It is possible to run up a bill of several thousands of dollars in a few days. (This is equally true if you are not ill but simply having a baby. This is a very expensive business and more difficult to insure yourself against too.)

If you need to call an ambulance, you should know that there is no unified national system for emergency calls, as there is in Britain. The best thing to do in an emergency is to phone the operator (see page 21).

calling an ambulance

As you might expect, ambulances in many areas of the USA are run by private companies and, yes, you have to pay for them too — and the cost might be anything from $10 to $100.

And once you have actually reached the hospital, be prepared for the first question to be not what is wrong with you but whether you can pay and who you are insured with, even if you are fairly obviously bleeding to death.

A good rule for travellers in the USA who are watching their expenses is: don't die. Funerals in America are enormously expensive, and 'morticians' are some of the biggest rip-off artists on the face of the earth. Americans have been persuaded to go in for embalming and for elaborate metal caskets rather than simple coffins, and there seems to be relatively little cremation. Funerals are most often conducted from schmaltzy, carpeted 'funeral homes', which have all sorts of elaborate lighting and trimmings. It is not unusual for several thousand dollars to change hands.

dying — American-style

You also have to *buy* your grave site, and there is no such thing as a funeral grant. Many people take out 'life' insurance, or join a 'burial society' so that their families can afford to pay for their funeral.

There is also a custom (which some may find gruesome) known as a 'visitation' or a 'viewing'. The night before the funeral, family and friends gather in the 'funeral home' to pay their respects to the deceased (and to look at the body in the open casket — and say how nice it looks). Often the casket will remain open until during the funeral service.

Don't go to the dentist in America unless you really have to. You will get excellent treatment, but you have to pay for this too, and costs can be extremely high.

dental treatment

There is a suspicion in the case of dentists, too, that treatment is prescribed when it is not really necessary. The first-time visitor to the USA rapidly gains the impression, for example, that one American teenager in two is wearing braces on his or her teeth.

Language: Understanding and Being Understood

For the English-speaking visitor to the USA language is obviously not the problem that it can be in many other countries. It can, however, cause difficulties, which is why this book has included, wherever appropriate, some help with terminology. (Conversations between Americans and visitors from Britain, Australia or New Zealand can also be a source of considerable interest and amusement because of the linguistic differences.)

In this section a few problematic points are dealt with that have not come up in the rest of the book.

everyday words with different meanings

Most British people — and Europeans who have learned British English — probably know that Americans call trousers 'pants' and pavements 'sidewalks'. There are, however, quite a few word differences that many visitors may not know about and may cause confusion. Here are just some of them.

billion	In American English this means a thousand million (1,000,000,000), not a million million.
cheap	To many Americans this word has strong overtones of 'cheap and nasty'; if they want to avoid this implication, they say 'inexpensive'.
homely	In American English this means 'not very good-looking', 'plain'. 'Homey' is used in the British sense of 'homely'.
momentarily	In American usage this may mean 'in a moment'. You will hear people saying, 'I'll do it momentarily'.
nervy	To Americans this means 'full of nerve' (i.e. courageous and/or cheeky).
pavement	In American English this means 'asphalt' or 'street covering'. Thus 'on the pavement' means 'on the road'.

presently	This can mean 'currently', 'right now', as well as 'in a short while' (as in British English).
quite	It is less usual in American than in British English for this word to mean 'not very'. For Americans, to say something is 'quite good' is not necessarily to damn it with faint praise; on the contrary, it means that it is 'rather good'.
scrappy	A 'scrappy' football game in the USA is a good game. It means something like 'a good scrap' (i.e. full of fight and competition).

British words which many Americans do not understand include 'queue' (they say 'line'), 'fortnight', 'spanner' (US: wrench), 'nought', and 'treacle' (US: molasses). And remember that Americans call the letter z 'zee'.

A number of Yiddish words are much more widely used and understood in America than in Britain. These include: **common Yiddish words**

schlemiel	a clumsy fool
to schlep	to carry with difficulty, to lug
schlock	rubbish, inferior goods, in bad taste.

Slang is a difficult subject to write about because much of it changes quite rapidly, and besides, American slang tends to become British slang after a while. It is, however, at the level of slang and colloquial vocabulary that most difficulties occur between British and American speakers. **slang**

Some differences are quite easy to cope with. For instance, in the USA at the moment 'gross' means 'in bad taste, offensive, disgusting, nasty', and to 'gross someone out' is to do or say something that he or she finds offensive or repulsive. Other things are harder to understand. Most Americans, for example, have not got the faintest idea what 'chuffed' means and are not familiar with 'off' meaning 'bad', 'sour' (as with milk). And there are other, less obvious problems. 'Cute' in the USA means what it does in Britain, but it can also mean 'good-looking', 'appealing' — so don't be offended if someone says you are cute. In America grown men can be cute as well as kittens. To 'wash up' means to wash yourself (washing up in the British English sense is called 'doing the dishes'). To 'knock someone up' in America means to make someone pregnant, so be careful how you use that. And to 'bomb' can mean to be a failure — the exact opposite of to 'go like a bomb'. 'Pissed' in American usage means the same as 'pissed off' and does not, in most parts of the country, mean 'drunk'. And 'fanny', to an American, means 'backside', male or female.

polite phrases Americans do not say 'please' and 'thank you' as often as British people do. They do, on the other hand, call people 'sir', 'ma'am' and 'miss' more often (see page 140). They also say 'Excuse me' when they mean 'Sorry'.

swear words Swearing in Britain and the USA is reasonably similar, although you may find some of the American forms interesting and colourful. American swearing is perhaps a little more anal than British, and 'Shit!' seems to be a milder expression than it is to the British. Americans do not use 'bloody' as a swear word, but some of them know that British people do and like to imitate it. They often, however, fail to appreciate how strong a swear word it is, so don't be offended if they use it on you.

forms of address In the USA you may encounter people with strange names like Mrs Frederick Smith. This does not mean that American women are called Frederick, merely that in some social circles it is considered the done thing for women to adopt not only their husband's surname but his first name as well. It is OK to refer to a woman as 'Joan Smith' but not as 'Mrs Joan Smith' — it has to be 'Mrs Frederick'. In other social circles this does not apply.

thanks When somebody thanks them for something, Americans almost always reply 'You're welcome' (or perhaps 'Sure' or something similar). They may find you impolite if you do not do the same.

dates Americans often say, for example, 'May third' and not 'May the third'. In writing dates — and this can cause confusion — Americans write month/day/year. Thus Christmas Day 1980 is 12/25/80 and *not* 25/12/80.

telling the time In telling the time a confusing American usage is 'It's ten of four.' This means 'ten minutes *to* four' (i.e. 3.50).

(Note that Americans typically write times with a colon
— 3:50.)

An American expressing 10.74 as 'ten-point-seventy-four'
is not showing invincible ignorance. It's just what
Americans say.

**working with
decimals**

Americans find it harder to understand British people
than vice versa, presumably because they have less practice. There are four times as many of them; they are
much less exposed to British accents on TV and in films;
and there are many more different British accents than
American accents. If you speak with a BBC accent, you
will probably be all right, but anything else can cause
problems, especially if people are not expecting a British
accent to begin with. (One gets the impression that wearing a label saying 'I AM BRITISH' (or Dutch, or whatever)
would be a good idea.) It is sensible to give people a
chance to get used to the way you talk by speaking a
little more slowly than usual at first.
   Americans are also totally incapable of distinguishing
between English, Australian, New Zealand and South
African accents. And they are quite likely to think that
Scots are from Mexico.

**making
yourself
understood**

Units of Measurement and Sizes

units of measurement	1 inch (in)		=	25.40 millimetres
	1 foot (ft)	= 12 in	=	0.30 metres
	1 yard (yd)	= 3 ft	=	0.91 metres
length	1 mile		=	1.61 kilometres
weight	1 ounce (oz)		=	28.35 grams
	1 pound (lb)	= 16 oz	=	0.45 kilogram
	1 ton		=	1.02 tonne

capacity	US	Imperial	SI
	1 pint (pt) (16 fl. oz)	0.83 pint	0.45 litre
	1 quart (qt) (2 pt)	1.66 pints	0.91 litre
	1 gallon (gal)	0.83 gallon ($6^2/_3$ pints)	3.64 litres

American gallons (and hence quarts and pints) are only five-sixths the size of Imperial gallons/quarts/pints.

Imperial	SI	US
1 pint (20 fl. oz)	0.57 litre	1.2 pints
1 quart	1.14 litres	2.4 pints
1 gallon	4.55 litres	1.2 gallons

calculating fuel consumption

Remember that each US gallon of petrol you buy will take you only five-sixths as far as an Imperial gallon — that is to say, you'll drive 20 miles on one US gallon when you might expect to drive 24 miles on one Imperial gallon, and 30 miles on one US gallon when you would expect to travel 36 miles on an Imperial gallon. Conversely, when your fuel gauge tells you that you are doing 20 miles to the US gallon, you are only doing 17 miles to the Imperial gallon.

cookery

measuring in cups and spoons

In American cookery books the cup is the standard measure. A cup contains half an American pint. When measuring liquids, therefore, you may use the following equivalents.

US		Imperial	SI
¼ cup (2 fl. oz)		one-tenth pint	57 millilitres
½ cup (4 fl. oz)	approx	one-fifth pint	0.11 litre
¾ cup (6 fl. oz)		one-third pint	0.17 litre
1 cup (8 fl. oz)		two-fifths pint	0.23 litre

Imperial	US	SI
¼ pint (5 fl. oz)	two-thirds cup	0.14 litre
½ pint (10 fl. oz)	1¼ cups	0.28 litre
¾ pint (15 fl. oz)	2 cups	0.43 litre
1 pint (20 fl. oz)	2½ cups	0.57 litre

Note that Imperial and US fluid ounces are *not* exactly the same.

With solid ingredients things are more complicated.

	US	Imperial	SI
butter/sugar/rice	2 cups	1 lb	0.45 kilogram
icing sugar	3 cups	1 lb	0.45 kilogram
flour	4 cups	1 lb	0.45 kilogram

The following approximate relationships hold between spoon measurements.

US	British	SI
1 tablespoon	1 tablespoon	20 millilitres/grams
2 tablespoons		
3 tablespoons	2 tablespoons	40 millilitres/grams
4 tablespoons		
5 tablespoons	3 tablespoons	60 millilitres/grams

Teaspoon measures (5 millilitres/grams) are approximately the same as they are in Britain.

No one has yet seen fit to devise an international system for sizing clothes. Even national systems vary enormously, so it's best to try things on if they catch your eye. However, here's a rough guide, which may be of some help if you go clothes shopping. (Under the 'other European' heading below the sizes specified are those for French/German/Scandinavian, Spanish/Portuguese and Italian clothes, in ascending order, but these are to be treated cautiously, as sizing is by no means consistent throughout Europe.)

women's clothes: approximate sizes

US	British	Other European
8	10	36/38/40
10	12	38/40/42
12	14	40/42/44
14	16	42/44/46
16	18	44/46/48
18	20	46/48/50

shoe sizes For British visitors to the USA calculating shoe sizes is relatively easy: you just add 1½ to the British equivalents. European shoe sizes, like those of clothes, are not uniform, but a rough guide is provided below.

women's shoes	US	British	Other European
	4½	3	35/36
	5	3½	
	5½	4	36/37
	6	4½	
	6½	5	37/38
	7	5½	
	7½	6	38/39
	8	6½	
	8½	7	39/40
	9	7½	
	9½	8	40/41
	10	8½	

men's shoes	US	British	Other European
	7½	6	39/40
	8	6½	
	8½	7	40/41
	9	7½	
	9½	8	41/42
	10	8½	
	10½	9	42/43
	11	9½	
	11½	10	43/44
	12	10½	
	12½	11	44/45
	13	11½	
	14	12	45/46

Meeting American People

The Americans are, on average, much more friendly and hospitable than the British and other northern Europeans, and much less inhibited. Americans are also inclined, as one British writer has put it, to be 'ruthlessly gregarious' and love to join clubs, organizations and societies.

It is therefore very easy — and enjoyable — to meet Americans. You can readily find a club that suits your interests if you want to, and you will in any case find that people in many places will simply start talking to you — whether you want them to or not.

You will notice that Americans get uncomfortable about talking to people unless they know their names. Almost every American will therefore rapidly tell you his or her name — and you are supposed to reciprocate. They will not rest, either, until they learn both your first name and your surname and know how to pronounce

Drawing by Ross; © 1984 The New Yorker Magazine, Inc.

them correctly. They will also want to know where you are from and what you do.

Men generally shake hands when introducing themselves (even if space does not really permit, as on a plane). Some women do, and some don't. Men in the USA are also much more likely than those in Britain to shake hands with close friends and family as a greeting or when taking their leave.

Americans are more likely than British people of the same age and social standing to use your first name. They may (with some regional variation) call you 'sir', 'ma'am' or 'miss'. These terms are often quite useful. For example, if you want to attract the attention of someone you do not know in Britain, you have to call 'Excuse me!', 'Hey!' or else cough loudly. In America you can call 'Sir!' or 'Ma'am!' instead.

If you are invited to stay in somebody's house, it is quite normal to take a present (Americans say 'gift') with you. You may choose a box of chocolates or something similar, or else a 'house gift', some small and not necessarily useful thing that can go in the house.

Americans come in many varieties. There is far more ethnic and social diversity in the USA than in most European countries. This makes it hard to generalize successfully about meeting American people, but it does make meeting Americans a varied and fascinating experience. Seeing the USA via films and TV does not really prepare the visitor for things like the extremes of poverty and wealth, for the extent to which the USA is peopled by non-Anglo-Saxons, or for the enormous range of political views, religious beliefs, personality types and lifestyles that one is likely to encounter. Nor does it prepare the foreigner for how much pleasure it is possible to derive simply from being together with Americans in America. If you have never been to the USA before, this book wishes you what Americans would doubtless also wish you if they knew you were coming: Have a nice trip!

Index

air travel 42—4
   see also baggage allowance; tickets
      and reservations
air-conditioning 15
   in buses 44—5
   in cars 28
   in homes 15, 95
   in motels 15, 54, 55
   in shops 87
airports 42—3
alcohol, laws relating to 47, 73—5
   see also drinks, alcoholic
ambulance, how to call 24, 131
animals, dangerous 18—19

bacon, American 59, 60, 62, 90
baggage allowance 2, 44
   see also luggage, checking in
bands, marching 114
banks, use of 8—11
   see also cheques; traveller's
      cheques
bar food 71—2
baseball 113, 115, 123—7
basketball 113, 115, 127
bathrooms 96—7
   see also toilets
beaches 112
bears, likelihood of encountering 18
beer 73, 75—6
bread, buying 71, 90—1
breakfast, in restaurants 54, 56,
      59—60
brunch 59
buses 81
   airport 4, 43
   long-distance 44—5

car, driving
   automatic transmission 28, 30,
      38, 40
   long journeys 38—40

road conditions 16, 19, 26, 29,
      40—1
   rules for 30—5
   in winter 40—1
   see also motorways; right side,
      driving on
car, hire of 26—9
   choice of model 27—8
   see also insurance, car
cellars 17, 98
censorship of TV 103
central heating 94—5
cheerleaders 114
cheques, use of 6, 8—10, 89—90
cinema 111—12
clothing
   buying 88—9
   sizes 88—9, 137—8
   suitable 15—16, 41
cocktails 60—1, 76—7
coffee 65—6
coins 7—8, 34
college and university 106—7
   sport 106, 113—14
   see also fraternities and sororities
cookers 97—8
cookery, measurements for 136—7
credit cards, use of 6—7, 10, 53
   for car hire 26
   loss of 6
   for petrol 6
curfew 83
curtains (US: drapes) 94
customs
   form 2, 3
   officer 3—4
cycling 49—51

dairy produce, buying 90
date, giving the 134
decimals, expressing 135
delicatessen food 71—2

dental treatment, high costs of
131
directions, finding, in towns and
cities 79—81
doctor, consulting 129—30
'doggy bags' 64
dollar notes (US: bills) 5, 7
double-glazing 95
drinks
alcoholic 60—1, 73—7
soft 38, 70—1, 78
see also alcohol, laws relating to;
beer; cocktails; wines,
Californian
'drive-ins' and 'drive-ups'
banks 9
fast-food bars 68
mail boxes 85
movies 111—12
driving licence 32, 75
drug stores 88, 129
dying, high costs of 131

educational system 105—7
electricity 92—4
emergency telephone calls 24, 35,
131

fast food 67—71
fish and chip shops 68—9
flag, devotion to 106, 108—9, 114
flannel, face, provision of 54, 96
football, American 113—14, 116,
120—3
fraternities and sororities 107
fruit and vegetables (US: produce),
buying 90

gambling
coins 8
laws on 108
garage sales 92
garbage see rubbish
graduation 106—7
guns, large numbers of 82—3

health, high costs of 128—31
see also insurance, health
high schools 105—6
hitch-hiking 48—9

holidays, national 109—10
hospitality 92, 96, 139—40
hospitals 130
'hot tubs' 98—9
hotels 24, 52, 53, 55
see also motels
humidifiers 16, 95
hurricanes 15

ice, frequent provision of 39, 55, 70
ice cream 70
ice hockey 113, 127
identification, proof of 5, 10—11,
75, 90
immigration 1—2
form 2—3
insects, control of 19, 95, 98
insurance
car, third-party 28
health 2, 128

jacuzzi 99

kitchens 97—8

language and terminology 132
clothing 88
driving 29
everyday 132—5
food 59—60, 62, 64, 68, 71—2
medical 129
sport 115—16, 126—7
Yiddish 133
see also manners, polite; slang;
swearing
lights and switches 93
limousine 43
locks
external 94
internal 94, 96
luggage, checking in 4, 44, 46
see also baggage allowance
lunch and dinner 60—6

mail see post box; post office
manners, polite 58—9, 134, 140
maps 39
measurement, units of 136—7
meat, buying 90
menus 62—4

milk, buying 90
motels 24, 52−5, 59
motorways (US: freeways) 29, 30,
        31, 34, 35−6, 41, 49
muffins, English 60, 68
mustard, American 64, 91

New York City 13
news coverage
        on radio 104
        on TV 100, 103
newspapers 111
non-smokers, arrangements for 44−5,
        47, 57

'panhandles' 13
parcel, posting 85
parking 33−5
passport 1−2, 4
        for identification 10, 75
patriotism 109, 114
        see also flag, devotion to
petrol consumption 37, 136
petrol stations (US: gas stations)
        37−9
        near motorways 36
        payment at 5, 7, 9−10, 37
pizza restaurants 69−70
plants, poisonous 19
plugs, electric 94
police 26, 32
        and guns 82
politics and TV advertising 102
post boxes (US: mail boxes) 84−5
post offices 84−5, 109
present (US: gift), giving of 140
pronunciation
        food and drink 70, 76, 77
        place-names 13−14
Public Broadcasting System (PBS)
        101, 102, 103

radio 18, 104, 120
rain check 115
religion 110−11
        evangelical Protestantism 103−4,
        110
restrooms see toilets
restaurants 56−71
        ethnic 66−7

        see also manners, polite
right side
        driving on 29−30, 50
        walking on 81
road conditions 16, 19, 26, 40−1
road signs 32−3
rubbish, disposing of 98

sales tax 58, 87
sandwiches 71−2
school buses 32
screens, insect 19, 95
sex, laws concerning 108
sharks, danger from 19
shopping hours 87
shops 87−91
shower (bathroom) 97
shower (gift) 112
sizes, clothing 88−9, 137−8
slang 133−4
snakes 18
soccer 117−20
        indoor 119
speed limit 30, 35
sport 113−27
        fixtures and results 116−17
        press coverage 118−20, 126
        professional 113−14, 117, 120
        school and college 106, 113, 114
        see also baseball; basketball;
                football, American; ice hockey;
                soccer; television
stamps, buying 84
subway 47−8
supermarkets 89
swearing 103, 134
swimming pools 55, 98

taps (US: faucets) 96−7
taxis
        at air terminal 4, 43
        do not like traveller's cheques 5
tea (drink) 65, 70, 97
telegrams 86
telephone system 20−5
        codes 21
        emergencies 24, 133
        international calls 23
        local calls 21
        long-distance calls 14, 21−2
        phoning from hotels 24

reversed-charge (US: collect) calls
    22−3
'toll-free' numbers 20, 24, 53
tones 20
television 15, 18, 100−4
    commercials 102
    programmes 103
    religious programmes 103−4
    and sport 113,117
    stations 100−1
tickets and reservations
    air 42
    bus 45
    train 46−7
time, telling the 134−5
time zones 14−15, 100
timetables 14
tips 53, 58
toilets, provision of 81−2
    on buses 44
    in motels 54
    at petrol stations 37−8
tokens, gift 88
tornadoes 15, 17, 98
traffic lights 30
trains 45−7, 81
trams 48

trash *see* rubbish
traveller's cheques (US: traveler's
    checks), dollar 5−6, 7, 8−9

underground 47−8

violence, level of, and safety 45, 48,
    82−3, 94
visa, tourist 1−2

waiters, waitresses 57−8, 62
walking 51
    on the right 81
Washington DC 13
water
    drinking, provision of 39, 57,
        87, 97
    heating of 96
weather 15−18
    forecasts 17−18
    spring and autumn 16−17
    summer 15−16
    winter 16, 40−1
wines, Californian 61, 77, 91

zip codes 84

Suggestions

This page can be used to send in your suggestions for improving the book. What vital matters have been overlooked? What difficulties and pitfalls have been neglected or glossed over? What else should the intending visitor know about the quirks of the American way of life? Please write and tell us.

If your suggestions are adopted in a future edition, you will receive a free copy in recognition of your services in helping other people cope with America.

═══════════════════════════════════════

Please send your suggestions to Peter Trudgill c/o Basil Blackwell Ltd, 108 Cowley Road, Oxford OX4 1JF.

Name . . . .

Address . . . .

. . . .

My suggestions are